BATTLE GROUND SOUTH ASIA

BATTLE GROUND SOUTH ASIA

PREM PRAKASH

Vitasta

Thank you for choosing a Vitasta book. For years we've been committed to publishing books that inform, inspire, and endure. Reach out to us for bulk purchases at preeti.vitasta@gmail.com Discover more titles at www.vitastapublishing.com

Published by

Renu Kaul Verma

Vitasta Publishing Pvt Ltd

C-29, Sector 7, Noida,

Uttar Pradesh - 201301

info@vitastapublishing.com

ISBN: 978-93-47098-60-4

First Edition 2026

MRP ₹ 495

Edited by Reena Singh and Vichitra Goel
Typeset by Shubhpreet Kaur
Cover Design by Smriti Maheshwari
Printed by Vikas Computer and Printers, New Delhi

Some men read history. A rare few live it, breathe it, and report it–one crisis at a time.

When the guns roared along the Himalayan ridges in 1962 and Indian soldiers fell in the frozen silence of NEFA, one journalist was there–not as a spectator, but as a witness to history in the making. When the subcontinent tore itself apart in the blood-soaked wars of 1965 and 1971, he was there again–notebook in hand, camera rolling, conscience unwavering.

Drawing on a career spanning over seventy-five extraordinary years, Shri Prem Prakash–founder of Asian News International (ANI), India's largest television news agency, and one of the most consequential journalists of the twentieth century–offers an unparalleled insider's account of the conflicts, crises, and geopolitical fault lines that have shaped South Asia's turbulent destiny.

From the catastrophic betrayal of 1962, when the nation clinging to *Hindi-Chini bhai bhai* was jolted by the reality of the Chinese aggression, to the thunder of artillery in the 1965 India-Pakistan War, to the birth of a new nation in 1971 forged in fire and sacrifice–Prakash takes the reader to the very frontlines of history.

These are not dispatches reconstructed from archives. These are memories etched in gunpowder and journalist courage.

A man who has interviewed every Indian Prime Minister from Jawaharlal Nehru to Manmohan Singh, who built a media empire from a singular resolve to project India's true voice to the world, and who has survived wars, emergencies, and the relentless churn of a changing nation–Prem Prakash writes not just as a journalist, but as the conscience of an era.

Battleground South Asia is essential reading for anyone who wishes to understand not just the wars raging today, but what India has become. It is not merely a book; it is a reckoning.

Because those who were there must tell us what the textbook never could.

–Dr Rajkumar Ranjan Singh

Former Minister of State for External Affairs of India

Contents

Preface

South Asia forms a major part of our planet, with the largest populated country, India, being a part of it. South Asia consists of countries such as India, Pakistan, Burma, Sri Lanka, the Maldives, Nepal, Bhutan, Bangladesh, and Afghanistan. Barring Afghanistan, most other countries were captured by the British when the Europeans moved towards Asia. This did not include Bhutan, which was a protectorate of the British. These highly civilised, ancient nations became a part of the British Empire. How these countries came to be ruled by the British is another story. Each fought for its freedom from British rule. Later, Bangladesh, a part of Pakistan, had to wage a war of liberation against Pakistan.

The failure of the Mutiny of 1857 did not stop the urge for independence from foreign rulers who had nothing in common with Indians. India achieved its independence after a long fight, both non-violent led by Mahatma Gandhi, and violent led by innumerable revolutionaries who sacrificed their lives. Though every sacrifice is invaluable, two names deserve special mention—Bhagat Singh and his colleagues, and Netaji Subhash Chandra Bose.

Netaji Subhash Chandra Bose led the Indian National Army of the Provisional Government of India as its President. With the support of Japanese troops, his Army reached Imphal towards the end of World War 2. At that crucial moment, America dropped two atomic bombs on Japan to force Netaji's ally to surrender. But the British will to stay on in India had been broken. Had the British been defeated by the Indian National Army in Imphal, there could have been a massive uprising in India in support of Netaji.

India became free on 15 August 1947. Tragically, it was divided into two countries. Thus, Pakistan was born—in two parts, East and West, carved out of India. A new country emerged in South Asia. Muhammad Ali Jinnah, its founding father, was the first Governor General of Pakistan and Liaquat Ali Khan, its first Prime Minister.

The reasons behind Pakistan's emergence and India's partition are another long story. The tragedy of poor relations between the two countries continues despite the wars of 1965, 1971 and 1999. Lord Mountbatten, who played a crucial role in the Partition, continued to be the Governor General of India with Jawaharlal Nehru as the Prime Minister and Sardar Vallabhbhai Patel as the Deputy Prime Minister.

Immediately after, India took up the task of framing a Constitution for the Indian Republic, demonstrating a great national effort by the founding fathers in the Constituent Assembly, presided by Dr Rajendra Prasad. India's well-known advocate, Dr B R Ambedkar, prepared the draft of the Constitution to be discussed and finalised by the Constituent Assembly. The Constitution was adopted on 26 November 1949, and came into force on 26 January 1950. The Republic of India was born. The country's relationship with the British Crown ended. However, India decided to remain in the Commonwealth of Nations despite being a Republic.

Burma, now Myanmar, was once a part of India. When the Sepoy Mutiny failed, the last Mughal Emperor, Bahadur Shah Zafar, was tried in the Red Fort and sentenced to imprisonment. The British sent him and some of his family and servants to the farthest corner of India to spend his last days in Rangoon. He died and lies buried there. The poet-emperor that he was, he wrote a couplet that best describes his faith in the people of India–

Ghazion mei bu rahe gee jab tak eeman ki
takht e London tak chale gee talwar Hindustan kee

(As long as there remains the scent of faith in the hearts of our Ghazis, so long shall the sword of Hindustan flash before the throne of London.)

India's revolutionaries and senior leaders fighting for the country's freedom were invariably sent to Mandalay, farther from Rangoon in Burma. Among them were Lala Lajpat Rai and Ajit Singh, uncle of Bhagat Singh. Burma was separated from India on 1 April 1937. Thereafter, the British built the obnoxious Cellular Prison in the Andaman Islands, where freedom fighters were sent and tortured.

With India's Independence in 1947, the powerful Indian Army that had helped the British rule their empire was dissolved. The great Buddhist country of Burma, home of the Shwedagon Pagoda, or the 'Golden Pagoda', became independent on 1 April 1948 and finally, sovereign, independent South Asia began to take shape. The first Prime Minister of Burma was U Nu, a great freedom fighter and democrat.

Japan had followed a friendly and strategic policy towards the countries it freed from European colonial rule in Asia. Having defeated and ejected the British from Burma, Japan invited Ba Maw to form a government for Burma. U Nu joined the government as Foreign Minister, but did not serve for long. Towards the end of the war, the British recaptured Burma.

U Nu and the great Burmese leader Aung San began

their agitation under the Anti-Fascist People's Freedom League. Tragically, Aung San who was only thirty-two, was assassinated together with six of his colleagues, including his brother, on 19 July 1947. This was a huge tragedy that hit Burma just as it was about to become independent. Its after-effects continue even today.

After India's independence, British Prime Minister Clement Attlee announced Burma's freedom, and it also became free on 4 January 1948. Its first President was Sao Shwe Thaik, and the first Prime Minister was U Nu.

Tragically, U Nu's rule did not last long as he was soon overthrown by General Ne Win, a trusted aide whom he had made a caretaker Prime Minister in 1958. General Ne Win imposed military rule on Burma on 2 March 1962. This has continued in one form or the other for several years. Aung San Suu Kyi, daughter of the legendary Aung San, who tried to bring democracy back, remains in detention in her own country and Myanmar continues to be under military rule.

Another event that brought a significant change in South Asia was when Jawaharlal Nehru decided to formally recognise the rule of Mao Tse Tung in China. Chiang Kai-shek, President of China, had been a great friend of India. During World War 2, he and his wife visited India to meet India's leaders, and urged the British to free India from British rule. Meanwhile, in China, Mao Tse Tung was zealously continuing his Communist revolution, resulting in Chiang's defeat. He was ultimately forced to withdraw his nationalist government to the island of Formosa (Taiwan). This resulted in mainland China being occupied and run by Mao. Several million Chinese were killed as Mao consolidated Communist rule in China. The United Nations continued to recognise the Republic of China as the Government of China under Chiang Kai-shek, though his area was restricted to the island of Formosa.

An immediate result of India recognising Mao's China was that Tibet lost its freedom. Did India consider this before recognising Mao's China? China had always considered Tibet as its own part. Ultimately, the Dalai Lama, the Head of Tibet, had to flee Lhasa and seek asylum in India, where he continues to live in exile.

Prime Minister Nehru had not consulted his cabinet or his Deputy Prime Minister Vallabhbhai Patel, who was in Bombay (now Mumbai), before recognising Mao's Government as the Government of China. Patel wrote a long letter to Nehru in protest and requested him to call an early meeting of the cabinet to consider the consequences of his recognition. Unfortunately, Vallabhbhai Patel passed away before this meeting could take place.

Historically, Indians have had a friendly attitude towards the people of China, though it has undergone a big change since the Chinese incursion in Ladakh and the 1962 war. Although Congress did not support

Britain's war effort during the second World War, it sent a medical mission under Dr Kotnis to help China in its war against Japan.

Unknown to India, China entered the Aksai Chin area of Ladakh and built a road there. Indian protests fell on deaf Chinese ears. Nehru had done his best to introduce Zhou Enlai and China to other countries despite opposition from the United States of America.

Nehru even encouraged China to participate in the Non-Aligned Movement.

Finally, the killing of Indian policemen while on patrol in Ladakh culminated in the India-China war of 1962. A heartbroken Nehru worked day and night to rebuild the Indian army and equip it with the latest weapons. He passed away on 27 May 1964, and was succeeded by Lal Bahadur Shastri.

Another incident that had a significant impact on South Asia was the early death of Muhammad Ali Jinnah on 11 September 1948, just a few days after he had completed his first year in office. He did not live to see the Constitution of the modern state of Pakistan as he had envisioned, after it was prepared and adopted by the Constituent Assembly of Pakistan.

Jinnah was succeeded by Khwaja Nazimuddin, another leader of the Muslim League who had migrated from India. Nawabzada Liaquat Ali Khan continued as Pakistan's Prime Minister.

Maj Gen Akbar Khan, Chief of Staff, attempted to gain power in Pakistan in 1951 by moving against Prime Minister Liaquat Ali Khan over the alleged mishandling of the Kashmir issue. However, the coup attempt failed. However, on 16 October 1951, Prime Minister Liaquat Ali Khan was assassinated while addressing a public gathering in Company Bagh area of Rawalpindi. The murderer was also shot dead on the spot. Till today, no one knows who was behind this killing. The two leaders who had dreamt of the state of Pakistan, Jinnah and Liaquat Ali Khan were gone, leaving the newly created country of Pakistan in a lurch.

The Constituent Assembly kept discussing drafts but failed to pass them. A second Constituent Assembly was then formed, and the Constitution for Pakistan was passed on 29 February 1956 and enforced from 23 March 1956. The Constitution proclaimed Pakistan as an Islamic Republic. This was not what Muhammad Ali Jinnah had wanted. Jinnah had envisioned Pakistan as a modern, inclusive state, where all citizens were equal, free to practise their religion and governed by the rule of law.

Eventually, Pakistan emerged as an Islamic state where the minorities were not equal. Consequently, Hindus, Sikhs and Christians who had stayed on in Pakistan soon began leaving the country. In 1947, Hindus and Sikhs formed 23 per cent of Pakistan's population, which at present has reduced to 2 per cent.

Civilian rule did not last long in Pakistan as Gen Ayub Khan soon seized power in a military coup against Iskander Mirza on 27 October 1958. Pakistan has been under military rule ever since.

Despite India's defeat in the 1962 war against China, Jawaharlal Nehru had managed to prevent Pakistan from undertaking any further military adventure with India. Gen Ayub Khan considered Nehru's successor, Lal Bahadur Shastri a weak leader, and saw an opportunity to attack India. He launched 'Operation Gibraltar' and had his army enter Kashmir in civil dress to incite the local population to rise against India. Little did he realise that the local population was reporting the presence of Pakistani troops in civil dresses to Indian authorities.

Failing in Operation Gibraltar, the Pakistani leader launched a military attack under 'Operation Grand Slam' to cut off Kashmir from India. The 1965 war between the two neighbours soon broke out in all its intensity. Lal Bahadur Shastri gave a free hand to the Indian forces to respond, and the Indian Army attacked Pakistan in Sialkot and Lahore, reaching the outskirts of these two major cities of Pakistan. Haji Pir in Kashmir, where this author climbed with the Indian Army, had already been captured. So were some more areas in Pakistan-occupied Kashmir.

Pakistan sought peace and accepted the UN resolution for a ceasefire, under which the Indian Army remained in possession of Haji Pir Pass in Kashmir, along with other areas, and held positions along the Ichhogil Canal outside Lahore and on the outskirts of Sialkot.

Afghanistan in the northern part of South Asia, extends from the high mountains of the Hindu Kush to its borders with Pakistan. Its history is as old as India's. It is believed that the early Vedas were written by the 'rishis' whose abode was what is today known as 'Rish Koh', the mountain of Rishis, near Kabul. Buddhism succeeded Hinduism, and the great relics from that period exist till date. Emperor Kanishk sent monks from there to China to spread the message of Lord Buddha.

Islam reached Afghanistan some fifty to seventy years before reaching Europe. Though sparsely populated, Afghanistan dwelled in peace with different tribes and clans, including Hindus. As a story goes, even when a family adopted Islam, the elder brother, known as 'Lala' in the local language, continued to be Hindu.

Under King Zahir Shah, Afghanistan was a progressive country, steadily moving towards the modern world, particularly in education, and for women from 1933 to 1973. The country also had French schools. Afghanistan's problems occurred in July 1973, when Daud Khan staged a coup with the help of the Communist Party of Afghanistan against King Zahir Shah while he was in Italy for medical treatment.

Afghanistan sided with the Soviets during the Cold War that the West, led by America, waged against the Soviet

Union. To wriggle out of this, Daud went strongly with the Non-Aligned movement, and scheduled a meeting of the Foreign Ministers of Non-Aligned countries in Kabul in April 1978, much to the dislike of the Soviet Union and the Communist Party. However, before the meeting could take place, a coup against him resulted in his whole family being killed, and the Communist Party taking control of the country under Nur Muhammad Taraki.

Another Communist leader, Hafizullah Amin, overthrew Nur Muhammad Taraki, suspecting him to be in touch with the Americans in early September 1979. Two months later in December 1979, the Soviets installed Babrak Karmal at the helm, overthrowing Amin. Babrak Karmal invited the Soviet troops to Afghanistan to stave off any American invasion. Thus began the downfall of Afghanistan.

Afghanistan now became the battleground between the Soviet Union and the United States, along with their allies, Pakistan and Saudi Arabia. The country is today ruled by Taliban, a fundamentalist Islamic group, where women's rights have suffered the most. However, the country's relations with India continues to be friendly.

Another turning point for South Asia was the birth of Bangladesh. In December 1970, the military rulers in Islamabad, supported by Zulfikar Ali Bhutto, refused to honour the results of the General elections, which would have made Sheikh Mujibur Rahman, leader of the Awami League in East Pakistan, the Prime Minister of Pakistan. The Punjabi military rulers did not accept a Bengali leader who had declared that the place of the army was in its barracks.

What followed was the army's crackdown on the people of East Pakistan under Gen Tikka Khan in March 1971. A huge tragedy struck people, with several million taking refuge in India. Pakistan attacked India in an attempt to stop it from helping the rebels in East Pakistan. The die was cast and it led to a war in December 1971, followed by the surrender of 93,000 Pakistan army men. It was the biggest surrender since World War 2. Bangladesh was thus born and West Pakistan now became simply Pakistan.

Sri Lanka, a beautiful island country, is inhabited by the Sinhalese and Tamils. The Tamils largely populate the north of the island, in and around Jaffna. The two communities lived peacefully during the British rule, but soon after independence, in 1948, the Tamils started facing discrimination from the government that was largely of the Sinhalese. Incidents of violence against the Tamils finally led to a demand for the separation and creation of a Tamil state in the north. This resulted in a civil war between the two, with a large group of Tamils led by V Prabhakaran under his organisation, the LTTE-Liberation Tigers of Tamil Eelam.

Around May-June 1987, the government of Sri Lanka imposed a blockade of the north denying the Tamils essential supplies, including food. India decided to come to their rescue and airdropped food and other supplies to the Tamils. The government of Sri Lanka took this as an interference in its internal affairs. Talks followed between the President of Sri Lanka J R Jayewardene and India's Prime Minister Rajiv Gandhi, culminating in a meeting on 29 July 1987 in Colombo.

An accord was duly signed on 30 July 1987, with India agreeing to help Sri Lanka end the conflict. Shortly after, when Rajiv Gandhi was witnessing a guard of honour by the Sri Lankan Naval contingent, an attempt on his life was made by Vijitha Rohana, a Navy officer. I was, at that point, walking beside the Prime Minister, covering the event. As Rajiv Gandhi was young and agile, he could save himself, taking the blow of the gun's butt on his shoulder. If it had hit his head, it could have been fatal. The accord saw a long fight in the northern part of Sri Lanka, where Indian forces had landed to help bring in peace, but instead had got bogged down in a fight with the LTTE.

The Maldives comprise of big and tiny islands spread across the Indian Ocean, extending to over 800 km from North to South and over 120 km from East to West. The capital of the Maldives, the island of Male, is 640 km away from Sri Lanka. Not all the islands of the Maldives are inhabited. The country is a popular tourist destination with its pristine white beaches. The sea is full of corals, not too far from the beaches. The beauty of its sea world needs to be seen to be believed.

Being almost on the Equator, the country remains hot and humid throughout the year and experiences a rainy season from May to August and again from December to March. The relief from extreme heat and humidity is limited during the monsoons, which brings dry mild winds as well.

The population of the Maldives comprises of people settling there from Sri Lanka and India. The early settlers were Buddhists, but Islam was adopted around 1153. Portugal also ruled over the islands for a while. The population is now entirely ethnic Maldivian, with Dhivehi as the spoken language. Islam is the state religion.

When the British took possession of Ceylon (now Sri Lanka) in 1796, the islands of Male, which was run by Sultans, became a British protectorate. The Maldives got independence from Britain in 1965, and in 1968, the Republic of Maldives was born. However, the British troops left only on 29 March 1976. Ibrahim Nasir was the first President of the country.

The Head of the State in the Maldives is now the President, assisted by a Vice President and a cabinet of Ministers. Elections are held on the basis of an adult franchise, and the elected representatives form the Majlis, a single legislature which, like most democracies around the world, has a five-year term.

India has been assisting the Maldives ever since its

independence and relations between the two countries had been cordial. With the rise of China's economic and military power, it has increasingly asserted itself in areas of Indian influence, including Sri Lanka and Maldives. China is using its financial powers to build infrastructure through loans rather than grants and Maldives today, is under a heavy debt, paying more than US $ 90.00 million to China every year, almost 10 per cent of its budget. It is feared that just as Sri Lanka had to give away its Hambantota port to China on a 99-year lease, the Maldives too may soon find itself in a similar situation.

Whether the current president of Maldives, Mohamed Muizzu will retain power in future elections is a big question. The Muizzu government signed a bilateral military pact with China on 5 March 2024, which resulted in deterioration of relations between the Maldives and India. Of late, President Muizzu has been making efforts to placate India. Only time will tell how India maintains its security in the Indian Ocean and whether Muizzu will retain power in the Maldives.

These events have changed South Asia in many ways, and continue to have their impact on the world.

A tragic massacre of tourists on 22 April 2025 at Pahalgam in Kashmir has changed equations again between India and Pakistan. India gave a strong response to the massacre of innocent tourists, launching Operation Sindoor on the night of 7 May 2025, to destroy key hideouts of Pakistan-supported Islamic terrorist groups.

In the four-day war that ensued, India succeeded in destroying the Chinese-built air defence operations of Pakistan, including its major air bases. Though a ceasefire had taken place, India refused to release water to Pakistan. All this, along with the active presence of China in South Asia, is bound to further change equations in the region.

The collapse of the Sheikh Hasina government was because of her refusal to cede St Martin's Island (also known as Daruchini Dwip) to the United States. The agitation against the Hasina Government, partly due to the way it functioned, was meant to bring about a regime change and install a pro-United States government.

Nepal also recently witnessed a massive agitation by the country's youth, resulting in the downfall of the K P Sharma Oli government which was sympathetic towards China. It is not clear which way the country is headed. The army has been asked to take control and restore peace in the country.

It is feared that South Asia may become a battleground for China's claim to world supremacy against the United States of America.

Chapter 1

In the twenty-first century world, South Asia is strategically placed among the divisive superpowers who wish to dominate the world. The end of the Cold War between the US-led West and the Soviet Union, was decided through a war fought in Afghanistan that eventually saw the Soviet Union break up. New equations have since emerged in the world with the rise of China as an economic and military power. The USA is trying to reassert its position as the world's number one country. Amidst all this, India's rise as a military power and as the world's fourth largest economy has given the country its own strength and position in the world.

Except for Bhutan and Afghanistan, all the South Asian countries were British colonies till the middle of the twentieth century, having lost their independence when the European powers began expansion towards Asia and Africa from the sixteenth century. The Asian nations they captured had a long history of success and high civilisation. When the Portuguese first came to the Court of Mughal Emperor Akbar, the Indian economy was flourishing and was the biggest in the world. The Portuguese had managed to block the entry of the English during Emperor Akbar's era. However, Thomas Roe, an ambassador for King James I of England, reached Emperor Jahangir's Court in 1615 and got his permission to start a trading business in India. Thus, the East India Company came into being.

Why was India taken in by these European businessmen appearing in the Mughal Court as ambassadors of their king? This question needs an answer, but suffice it to say for the moment that the Mughal Emperor was fully aware of his power and confident that these foreign traders could do no harm. Why these traders were permitted to have their own security personnel, which ended up as an army, is yet another perplexing question. The Mughals had a system of policing to maintain law, order and peace in the country, which could well have protected these foreign traders and their factories. Why the Mughal administration gave in to their request does not have any logical answer.

The tragedy of the rich and powerful Mughals in India lay in the system used to administer the vast empire they had created, a system that did not function properly and was corrupt at each level. As Thomas Roe described in his book *The Embassy of Sir Thomas Roe to India*, his journey from Surat to Agra involved keeping corrupt officials at bay through gifts or other means. At the end of his journey, he was barely left with any presents for the Mughal Emperor and other important dignitaries.

The East India Company made its first expansion in South India from Madras (today's Chennai). They bought a large piece of land along the coast and developed Fort St George. It was a self-contained area, which is still in use, with some offices of the Tamil Nadu government. As habitation expanded beyond the Fort, it grew into the city of Madras. It must be remembered that the Indian population was smaller back then, and so were cities and villages.

In South India, the East India Company did not face any interference from the Mughal administration. The Company's business flourished in Madras before expanding all over South India. Seeing the success of their venture in Madras, the East India Company bought a large piece of land on the banks of the Hooghly River, near Kolkata, and built Fort St William along with other trading infrastructure. This significantly contributed to the expansion of the East India Company, which, in due course, became a state in the guise of a trading establishment.

The last powerful Mughal Emperor was Aurangzeb, who was unpopular among the Indians. One Friday, he could not go to Jama Masjid in Delhi for his Friday prayers, as the local people were demonstrating against his ban on music, imposition of *Jizya* tax on Hindus and other extremist policies. He then decided to build a mosque, the Moti Masjid, inside the Red Fort. There was no mosque within the Fort until then.

Aurangzeb spent virtually all his life fighting opposing forces. The East India Company smartly stayed out of his way all this while. However, the East India Company's navy came into conflict with a Mughal warship escorting pilgrims to Mecca and was defeated. Aurangzeb, thereby, imposed heavy penalties on the Company and its officers. They had to seek apology by squatting on the ground in the open court, thus surviving the possibility of expulsion from India.

Aurangzeb passed away at the age of eighty-three. His successors could neither manage the vast empire that he had built nor control the corrupt Governors in the provinces. The downfall of the once powerful, rich Mughal Empire had begun. The Governors in the provinces were neither reporting properly nor sending money to the Centre. Fed up with them, Shah Alam decided to grant the Diwani rights (tax collection) to the East India Company. The East India Company thus became the de facto ruler of Bengal, Bihar and Orissa.

The grant of Diwani rights increased the influence of the Company all over India. The Company now forced itself into a monopoly in these three states. The Company began to strengthen its army, and faced no financial problems in doing so. The Company's revenues had increased multifold. All this happened because of one corrupt Governor of Bengal, Mir Jafar, who did not send money to the Mughal Emperor at the Centre in Delhi.

Even as the East India Company expanded its business activities, it began capturing territories with conquests made by its powerful large army. The Company staff began looting India. On capturing an area, they would keep a fair amount of gold, jewellery and money for themselves instead of giving it to the Company.

Some of this wealth—diamonds and jewellery—is on display at the Tower of London, in the United Kingdom. The famous Koh-i-Noor diamond, broken into two by the British, is also on display here along with several thousand other gemstones, diamonds and jewellery, most of it looted from India. A bulk of the loot is also on display at several of the country homes of former sires, which are now under the management of the National Trust of the UK Government as most of the successors of the original owners could not pay inheritance tax on the high values of the property and the riches they left behind.

A great weakness of the East India Company staff, including senior officials, was their discriminatory, racist attitude towards their subjects, the Indians. The Indians could neither tolerate this, nor could they escape it. They considered Englishmen inferior, as people who traded humans as slaves. The English would capture Africans and sell them to the Americans in England who treated them cruelly. Some were brought to India and sold to the Mughal Emperors, as well as to kings in the smaller states. Unlike the Americans, the Indians treated these men and women from Africa as humans.

The British managed to crush the Sepoy Mutiny of 1857 when the sepoys rebelled against the foreign rulers. After crushing the Mutiny, the British made efforts to win the confidence of the Indians.

The first task for the British officials to win the confidence of the Indians was to make the country safe and establish law and order. The second was to provide education by running a number of primary schools and offering free education. Christian missionaries opened many more schools. Next on their list was providing healthcare by opening government hospitals that offered free treatment to the poor. Finally, they had to provide justice in matters of litigation. The system seemed to work fine, till it came to dealing with freedom fighters, who were charged with sedition and given the death sentence.

The First World War in 1914 made the British realise the importance of the Indian Army in protecting their interests and their country. The Indians fought bravely in many places, especially in France, and made huge sacrifices. The wounded were brought to England and treated by British doctors and nurses. The soldiers served without any discrimination. However, their officers were unhappy that English nurses served the Indians. When restored to health, the soldiers went around the city and a few even wrote back to their friends back home that the English girls were no better than ours! A certain wall had been broken and Indians came to know what England was all about.

In India, there was an English officer, Allan Octavian Hume, whose loyal Indian staff protected him during the Mutiny of 1857. His analysis of the Mutiny included, among other reasons, the Company's failure to take even these friends into confidence and give them positions in the government. He was also aware that many Englishmen who had made India their home felt that they, along with loyal Indians, should have a role in governance. Thus, came into being the Indian National Congress, founded by Hume, Dadabhai Naoroji, Surendranath Banerjee and others on 28 December 1885, with the objective of establishing home rule. The ruling Englishmen did not approve of the idea at all. Nevertheless, Congress was born.

Over time, the party saw another three Englishmen evincing interest in the President's post. Other senior Indians were also active now, including Bal Gangadhar Tilak, Muhammad Ali Jinnah, Badruddin Tyabji, Subramania Iyer, R C Dutt, Lala Lajpat Rai, and Bipin Chandra Pal among others. Though Congress remained active, it was more of a debating club. However, Mohandas Karamchand Gandhi's arrival in India from South Africa on 9 January 1915 changed that. He had led a non-violent agitation against apartheid in South Africa. Before engaging in Congress, he undertook an India-wide tour to see the condition of the country and its people.

The Congress was destined to undergo a sea change when Gandhi began to take action. Besides negotiating with the British, he launched a movement to highlight the problems in the country. That led to differences of opinion with some of the then leaders of the Congress, including Muhammad Ali Jinnah. In contrast to Gandhi's non-violent Satyagraha, Jinnah felt this approach would backfire on an independent India as unions would resort to Satyagraha to force their demands on the government. His fears were well-founded. Jinnah resigned from the Congress. It is a pity that neither Gandhi nor other senior leaders of the party made any attempt to prevent Jinnah from leaving. It left him bitter towards a party he had helped build.

Gandhi agreed to support the British in the First World War hoping that they would grant home rule to India after the war. This was Congress's main demand. However, after the war, some other colonies, like Canada and Australia, were permitted home rule as dominions of the United Kingdom. India's demand was dismissed, as it was said that the country was not ready yet. Already impoverished, India was charged for the expenditure incurred by the British on the First World War. This was unfair as it was Britain's war in Europe, not India's.

Gandhi was shocked when the British denied self-rule to India. With no alternative left, he started a non-violent struggle against British rule. Meanwhile, the revolutionaries, recovering from the defeat of the Mutiny of 1857, were active once again. They had never accepted the idea of home rule. For them, a great nation with an ancient civilisation like India had to rise on its own. They demanded complete independence.

The long freedom struggle saw hundreds of young people fighting for the country's independence and embracing the gallows with a smile. Within the Indian National Congress, Subhas Chandra Bose was elected as President of the Congress. Though he deeply respected Gandhi, he did not have much faith in his policy of non-violence. Bose was brilliant and had passed the exam for the Indian Civil Services. Bose went to England for training, but resigned without joining. He was a man of high principles, and returned the amount the British might have spent on his training for the ICS.

The rise of Hitler in Germany saw Europe get into another war. In the Pacific area, differences between Japan and the USA brought the two nations to war. Japan was already fighting in China. Subhas Chandra Bose reached Japan, where another revolutionary, Rash Behari Bose, was waiting for him, having raised a small Indian National Army. He then handed over that role to Netaji, as Subhas Chandra Bose later came to be addressed. A Provisional

Government of Free India was proclaimed under Netaji's Presidency. This government was recognised by eight nations, including Japan, and became independent India's government in exile.

The end of the Second World War saw the Indian National Army reach Imphal. A bitter fight between the INA and British forces, supported by the USA and its air power, resulted in the INA's defeat. Around the same time, the USA detonated two nuclear bombs over Hiroshima and Nagasaki, forcing Japan to surrender.

Netaji was travelling to Tokyo in a converted Japan air force bomber along with senior Japanese officials when he arrived at Formosa for the plane to refuel. The next morning, when the overloaded bomber took off, it crashed. Netaji suffered serious injuries and died in Formosa. Habibur Rahman who was travelling with Netaji survived. This tragedy had immeasurable consequences that hit India's future. The country was inching towards independence, and the battle at Imphal, gave Britain a strong message that it would not be able to rule over India much longer.

Meanwhile, Britain elected a new government of Prime Minister Clement Atlee who defeated the wartime leader, Winston Churchill. The new Labour Party government decided to leave India. Clement Attlee announced that irrespective of whether Indian leaders from different parties unanimously agreed to take charge of the country or not, Britain would leave India on 30 June 1948.

Independence finally came to India on 15 August 1947, but the country saw a partition. A new country, Pakistan, was carved out on 14 August 1947 with Muhammad Ali Jinnah as its Governor General. This major event brought a huge change in South Asia.

The independence of India and emergence of an independent Pakistan also set in motion the end of British colonialism in South Asia. The rule of Britannica was ending.

Chapter 2

Pakistan was carved out of what was once India. Muhammad Ali Jinnah and other leaders of the Muslim League reached Karachi, waiting for Lord Louis Mountbatten to arrive and formally declare independence for the new country of Pakistan. The Constituent Assembly members of the new country had assembled in Karachi on 10 August.

Jinnah was unhappy that Pakistan was torn into two parts, separated by the expansive India. He had no alternative as Lord Mountbatten had already conveyed on behalf of the British government that this is what Pakistan will be, or he could forget about it. He had to accept the Pakistan that the British offered him.

Jinnah's problem was that the majority of the population of Pakistan lived in the Eastern part and spoke Bengali. West Pakistan comprised the provinces of Punjab, the NWFP (North-West Frontier Province), Sindh, and

Balochistan, each with its own language and distinctive culture. Balochistan had been an autonomous state and was ruled by the Khan of Kalat. The NWFP was not interested in being a part of Pakistan, but was forced by the British to be a part of them when they were denied their own separate country, Pakhtunistan. Punjabi-speaking Punjab was the majority province in West Pakistan.

The power base of both Muhammad Ali Jinnah and Nawabzada Liaquat Ali Khan was among the Urdu-speaking Muslims in UP, home of Liaquat Ali, or in Gujarat and Mumbai for Jinnah, and among the Muslims of Bengal. Their entire base of supporters had now been left behind in India. Though several million Urdu-speaking Muslims had migrated to Pakistan, they were the majority in Sindh and Punjab, where they were known as 'muhajirs'. Neither of the provinces had had the Muslim League government before independence.

Soon after independence, like other princely states, the Khan of Kalat sought accession to India. This was denied by Jawaharlal Nehru who argued that India could not protect Kalat as Balochistan was not within Indian territory. While Balochistan would have been largely surrounded by Pakistan, it did have access to the sea at Gwadar. Nehru also ignored the fact that East Pakistan, though surrounded by India and the sea, was under the Pakistan government based in Karachi, the capital of Sindh.

G M Syed, the great leader of Sindh, publicly

expressed the desire that Pakistan would not disturb the Sindhi culture or language. He was soon disillusioned by the way the Muslim League went about imposing the Urdu language on the region. Dismayed by Pakistan's emergence after 14 August 1947, and the manner in which the Muslim League leaders, who did not belong to any of the provinces making up Pakistan, were treating the people, G M Syed led a movement asking for the creation of the independent nation of Sindhudesh.

West Punjab was the largest province of West Pakistan and its Punjabi-speaking population was the backbone of the Pakistan army. The British had a strange attitude towards India's people, labelling them as 'a martial race', especially the Punjabis. In Pakistan, the Punjabis dominated its army. Being the largest province in West Pakistan, the Punjabis thought of themselves as the rulers of Pakistan, forgetting that East Bengal was also a part of Pakistan and that it had more people than all the provinces of West Pakistan put together.

Jinnah had never been popular in the NWFP and all his efforts in that region before independence had met with failure. Now was the time for him to deal with the leaders of the Congress party in the NWFP. Congress had been very popular in the NWFP where it ran the provincial government. The brave Pashtuns, virtually worshipped Khan Abdul Ghaffar Khan, who came to be known as Frontier Gandhi. His followers wore red shirts and were known as *Khudai Khidmatgar* (servants of God). At the time of independence, the provincial government was run by Dr Khan Sahib, the younger brother of Khan Abdul Ghaffar Khan. He refused to resign despite being pressurised by the Governor of the NWFP, Sir George Cunningham, who was Jinnah's choice for the job.

All efforts by Muhammad Ali Jinnah before Partition to establish a base for the Muslim League in the province which had 95 per cent Muslim population had failed.

A large part of the population lived in the Pashtun areas annexed by Maharaja Ranjit Singh after his victory over Afghanistan. This also included the city of Peshawar and its surrounding valley. The city used to be the winter capital of Afghanistan when Kabul was covered by snow. The Pashtun areas on both sides of the road from Khyber Pass to the border with Afghanistan were as good as independent. No writ of the British rulers ran there. Moreover, they hated the Muslim League government in Pakistan after independence.

The people living in the Pashtun areas were divided among various tribes. The British used to placate them through a political agent who would meet the tribal heads and give them large sums of money as an annuity.

As the NWFP had a Congress government, the Muslim League did not have any support in the province. Lord Mountbatten, therefore, called for a referendum to let the people decide whether they wanted to be a part of Pakistan or India. It was a strange choice as the NWFP would have been a landlocked province of India. Khan Abdul Ghaffar Khan demanded a third choice to be included—Pashtunistan, an independent Pashtun country, but Lord Mountbatten turned it down.

This created an impasse between the British government, represented by Lord Mountbatten, and the NWFP ruled by the Congress party. With the Governor of the NWFP being pro-Jinnah, Khan Abdul Ghaffar Khan and the Congress party expected the referendum to be rigged and opted to boycott it. Many opined that this boycott was like offering the NWFP on a platter to Pakistan, and publicly appealed to the Frontier Gandhi to reverse his decision.

The call for a boycott did have its impact, and only 50 per cent of the eligible voters turned out to cast their votes. Many Hindu and Sikh voters had left for India, and those living there were also absent from the referendum because of the boycott call. When the result of the referendum was announced on 20 July 1947, three days after the poll, those who voted for Pakistan secured 50.48 per cent of the total votes polled, while 49.52 per cent voted against Pakistan. The vote in favour of joining Pakistan was thus decided by a mere 0.48 per cent, or only a few thousand votes. There were serious allegations of rigging by Governor Cunningham, under whose aegis the referendum was held. Cunningham was close to Jinnah.

Dr Khan Sahib's government refused to accept the rigged result and refused to resign. The Governor General of India, Lord Mountbatten, too did not advise the Governor to dismiss Dr Khan Sahib's government. Amidst these charges of rigging, he could have well asked for a repoll and it was believed that the votes then would have gone in favour of making the NWFP a part of India.

The majority of the Muslims who came from India to Pakistan spoke Urdu as it was their language in UP. There was little migration of Muslims from other provinces of India to East Pakistan, apart from Bihar. In British India, Urdu was studied in most Northern provinces. The Muslims of UP who migrated to Pakistan arrived there in Sindh via Rajasthan while others went to Punjab, mostly to Lahore. People in the provinces that now made up Pakistan realised that they were ruled by leaders who were not from any of their provinces. Jinnah was an exception as he was regarded as the leader of Muslims in undivided India, even though the Muslim League had failed to win in any Muslim-majority province in the 1937 elections. Before Independence, Muslims opposing the Partition had clearly declared that Jinnah was not their leader.

The Muslims who went to Pakistan from India were labelled as 'Muhajirs'. They are classified under a different caste of Muslims in Pakistan, like Shias and Sunnis. I remember speaking to a Pakistani diplomat whose parents had moved from India to Pakistan. He had said to me,

'Prem Bhai, I have a problem when my children ask why they are known as Muhajirs? I cannot give them a convincing reply apart from telling them that it's because our ancestors had moved from India.'

From personal experience, I can vouch that many of those who went to Pakistan were not happy. Delhi and Lucknow are known for its culture, its *tehzeeb*. They missed it among the people of Punjab and Sindh. In Lahore in 1961, I had stayed in a hotel where the owner had come from Delhi. He had been eagerly waiting for the three of us journalists from India who were to stay there. He could not believe that we were visiting Pakistan—'*mulk jahan tehzeeb nahi hai*,' (a country where there is no culture). He had gone on a tirade against Pakistan and said what a mistake he had made leaving Delhi.

India has far more languages and dialects. Apart from English, fifteen languages are printed on its currency notes. The Hindus, Sikhs and Christians who had come from Pakistan have settled well as locals in different states of India without any discrimination. India's Constitution and its lively democracy have ensured this.

The Constituent Assembly of Pakistan was formed by drawing members from the existing legislative assemblies that made Pakistan. Many members were nominated. The Assembly had its first meeting on 10 August 1947.

Quaid e Azam Muhammad Ali Jinnah addressed the Constituent Assembly on 11 August 1947 to talk about his vision for Pakistan. The address, the preamble for their country, was meant to guide them in framing their Constitution. He stressed on several points, including telling the members that all the citizens of Pakistan would be equal before the law. He added that in the course of time, Hindus would cease to be Hindus and Muslims would cease to be Muslims, not in the personal religious sense, but as citizens of the state. Was he pronouncing Pakistan to be a secular state?

He stressed that law and order would protect the life, property and beliefs of all. Clearly, he was not visualising a state where minorities would be discriminated against by the majority Muslim population or by the country's law and order agencies. He envisioned an inclusive and impartial government that ensured equality to its people. He visualised a modern country in the Islamic world, much like the Turkey of Mustafa Kemal Atatürk.

He expected the people to forget and forgive what had happened in the recent past—the riots and massacres—and stand united as equal citizens of the new State. He urged the members to ensure that the evils of bribery, black marketing and nepotism, now known as corruption, did not exist in the new State.

Taking charge of the new country from the British on 14 August 1947 as Governor General, and his deputy, Nawabzada Liaquat Ali Khan as Prime Minister, the government did set out on its work. However, Jinnah did not live long enough to see the country of his dreams take shape. He had been a patient of tuberculosis, a fact not known to many, and his health did not allow him to take on the responsibility of providing stability to the new country.

Despite his failing health, Jinnah was travelling to different provinces to meet the people and the local leaders. He went on a tour to Dhaka on 19 March 1948 to meet the local leaders and inform them of the progress being made to stabilise the new country. In his address to them on 21 March 1948, he declared that Urdu was to be the national language of Pakistan. Proud of their language and culture, the Bengalis reacted to this immediately. They considered that Urdu was being forced on them to destroy their culture and language. Protests followed even as Jinnah returned to Karachi.

Jinnah's visit to East Pakistan had been a disaster, as had been his earlier visits to the provinces in West Pakistan. In East Pakistan, language-based riots soon broke out and the people could not be placated. The government tried to control these riots and protests by declaring them unlawful. Trouble in East Pakistan further escalated when several students were killed in police firing during a demonstration in 1952.

Life had not been easy for the Muslim League leaders, who came from India. Jinnah and his sister, Fatima, who played a major role beside him were from Gujarat.

Prime Minister Liaquat Ali Khan was from UP. Many of his followers had moved to Pakistan, but they now all known as 'muhajirs' (refugees) by the locals despite being Pakistani. Their language in UP was Urdu. Karachi was a part of Sindh and Sindhi was their local language. The majority of East Pakistan spoke Bengali and they were not prepared to give up Bengali for Urdu.

There are several controversies about how Jinnah felt about Pakistan once it became a reality. Much has been written about it by various historians.

Let me sum it up by quoting Alex von Tunzelmann from her book *Indian Summer: The Secret History of the End of an Empire*. She writes, 'On 11 September 1948, Muhammad Ali Jinnah finally succumbed to his illness. He had been on his way to Karachi, Fatima remembered him speaking in delirium, "Kashmir…Give them….the right…to decide…Constitution…I will complete it…soon…Refugees…give them all assistance…Pakistan." According to his doctor, Jinnah saw Liaquat and told him that Pakistan was 'the biggest blunder of my life'. Further, he declared, 'If I now get an opportunity, I will go to Delhi and tell Jawaharlal to forget about the follies of the past and become friends again'. It is impossible to prove whether Jinnah actually said these words or not; either way, he was to have no further opportunity for a rapprochement.

It is strange to learn that the ambulance of Pakistan's Governor General broke down on its way to his house.

Moreover, it took an hour to get another ambulance while the Head of the State of Pakistan lay critically ill, suffering in the heat and humidity on a busy road. His sister Fatima has said that finally on reaching the house, he slept for two hours, but when he woke up he took her leave and went into eternal sleep. He was buried the next day at Mazar e Quaid.

The Constitution of the country of Jinnah's dreams had still not been prepared. He was no longer there to guide the Assembly on making the Constitution. He had left behind a Constituent Assembly of quarrelling members.

Nawabzada Liaquat Ali Khan, the Prime Minister, now had the responsibility of seeing the new country take firm roots. He was a lawyer by profession before joining the Muslim League. However, soon attempts were made to dislodge him; an attempt on his life was made in March 1951. It was said to have been instigated by someone in the army and certain left-wing politicians who opposed him. However, he did not live long, for a few months later, on 16 October 1951, he was shot dead by an unknown person while addressing a public meeting in Rawalpindi.

Two towering leaders, who had achieved their dream of getting Pakistan from the British, were gone.

Pakistan soon elected a second Constituent Assembly, and on 29 February 1956, the Constitution was passed proclaiming Pakistan to be an Islamic Republic, something that Jinnah had not wanted.

Pakistan had staggered on with far too many changes in leaders between Liaquat Ali's assassination and the rise of Iskander Mirza on 23 March 1956 and ironically, till the Constitution was passed, Pakistan had continued as a dominion of the British crown. Thus, Iskander Mirza became the first President of Pakistan. However, his government, even though it had a constitution, could not control unrest in the country or bring about stability.

Having abolished the post of the Prime Minister in 1956, President Iskander Mirza took charge of the country himself, but failing to control the unrest in the country through police forces, he imposed Martial Law on 7 October 1958. Gen Ayub Khan was given the charge of Martial Law. The General, however, delivered a final blow to end civilian rule and overthrew Iskander Mirza on 27 October 1958 in a coup. Thus, began Military rule in Pakistan, which has continued ever since in one form or another. Pakistan has the dubious distinction of being the first country in South Asia to go under military dictatorship.

Gen Ayub Khan was challenged by Fatima Jinnah, Muhammad Ali Jinnah's sister, when she decided to contest against him in the Presidential elections on 2 January 1965. She could not bear to see the legacy of Muhammad Ali Jinnah being destroyed like this and Pakistan being brought under military dictatorship and was keen on restoring Pakistan to the vision of its founder, Muhammad Ali Jinnah.

She travelled to East and West Pakistan, campaigning for her election and informing the people of what lay ahead if military rule continued. Though she won the popular vote, she was not declared as President of Pakistan. There were allegations of manipulation and rigging by the military through an Electoral College that could overrule the popular vote. This consisted of about 80,000 so-called 'basic democrats'—Gen Ayub Khan's clever ploy to remain in power. Fatima Jinnah was denied the post for which the people of Pakistan had voted. This ended all hopes of restoring democracy, and paved the way for the first military dictatorship in Pakistan which has continued ever since.

With the advent of military dictatorship, the Anglo-American power axis achieved their objective of the kind of Pakistan that would toe their line. Pakistan became the frontline state to serve their interests in the Cold War that later turned hot in Afghanistan. A secret American air base was established in Peshawar, from where U-2 aircrafts flew over the Soviet Union to monitor their nuclear and space programmes. Meanwhile, the ordinary citizens of Pakistan continued to suffer from poverty and lack of education.

Chapter 3

Soon after Independence, the Constituent Assembly of India worked on framing the Constitution for the Republic of India. The founding fathers ensured that the Assembly represented all interests of India and was truly a national body. The draft was prepared by one of India's most learned advocates and a representative of the marginalised, Dr B R Ambedkar. The Assembly was presided over by the learned, Dr Rajendra Prasad, a Congress leader. Following Gandhi's advice, the Assembly represented all the national parties, and the Nehru government included leaders from other parties during the transitional period while the Assembly framed the Constitution. The Constitution of India was unanimously adopted by the Assembly on 26 November 1949.

The Republic of India was proclaimed on 26 January 1950 because it was on the same date in 1930 that the Congress declared *Purna Swaraj* or complete independence, as its goal against its earlier demand for Home Rule or dominion status. This was the goal of young revolutionaries like Bhagat Singh and his colleagues. The popularity of the Congress and Gandhi was negatively affected during the trial of these young revolutionaries in Punjab. To regain this lost confidence, the Congress adopted the goal of these revolutionaries as that of the nation.

Soon after the Constitution was adopted, preparations began for India's first elections for the government. So the first priority was forming an independent Election Commission. A senior bureaucrat, Sukumar Sen, was appointed to set up the Commission and conduct the elections for 489 seats of the Lok Sabha. The elections began from 25 October 1951 and went through different phases before ending in February 1952. It was a mammoth task, covering regions from the desert state of Rajasthan to Ladakh, high up in the Himalayas.

Sukumar Sen, who remained the Chief Election Commissioner till December 1958 carried out the task successfully. The Indian National Congress, led by Jawaharlal Nehru, secured 364 seats, followed by the Communist Party of India who won sixteen seats. The remaining seats went to other smaller parties. Unfortunately, there was no leader in the Opposition as none of the other parties secured enough seats to claim that position.

Jawaharlal Nehru was sworn in as the Prime Minister of the Republic of India. The country had successfully transitioned into a democratically governed nation. This showed the way to the rest of South Asia, demonstrating that with will, determination, and belief in democratic values, countries can ensure people's participation in government formation. India's people and its leaders had shown their maturity to the world by ensuring that every section of society was a part of the Constitution-making process. The country had established an impartial and independent Election Commission that paved the way for the formation of the government.

Then began the long and hard work of rebuilding India. Sardar Vallabhbhai Patel took charge as Deputy Prime Minister and Minister for Home. The Constitution of India empowers the states to maintain law and order in their areas. Overall, it is the responsibility of the Ministry of Home Affairs to ensure that the country remains at peace. Contrast this stable period to the dark period of instability with no law and order that the country went through when the Mughal Empire weakened and the East India Company took over India's administration. It is worth noting how relieved the Indian people must have felt when law and order was restored in the country.

When India gave recognition to Mao's China on 1 April 1950, it was among the first few nations to recognise Communist China. The recognition had far-reaching consequences as Tibet lost its independence because China had always considered Tibet to be a part of China. India's international borders with Tibet had always been peaceful. The Maharaja of Jammu & Kashmir, whose state touched Tibet's border in Ladakh, had never felt the need to set up a border post. How and why India ignored this aspect has never been explained.

Nehru did not consult his cabinet before taking the action. The British had left behind a strong intelligence network across Tibet. The Indian Army also had a small contingent stationed in Xinjiang province of China, bordering Tibet. This too was withdrawn because of the recognition given to Mao's China. India had weakened its strategic importance by giving up its foothold and dominance in Tibet. Did the government consider the huge disadvantage the country would face in future relationships with China by giving up this position of strength?

India continued to overlook Ladakh even after recognising Communist China. The country failed to set up any border outposts, as its international border in this area was now with China. The Chinese took full advantage of this lapse and quietly built a road in Aksai Chin area of Ladakh, which served as a short cut to Tibet. When India protested, the Chinese laid claim to the area. When the Indian Ambassador met the Chinese Premier to lodge a protest, he is said to have replied, 'Where were the Indians in the area?'

After assuring the Dalai Lama that he would intercede on his behalf, Nehru planned a visit to Lhasa after consultation with Chinese Premier Zhou Enlai. The Chinese Premier had assured Nehru of a welcome in Lhasa. However, the visit was later cancelled when China declared that the situation in Lhasa was not conducive to the Indian PM's visit.

Thus, despite India's best efforts, relations between India and China deteriorated. The Dalai Lama had to flee to India in March 1955 to avoid being deposed or arrested by China. The Dalai Lama's journey from his Potala Palace residence to India with his family, and government officials, was not an easy task. The Dalai Lama's people, assisted by the Indian officials who knew Tibet well, handled the task well. All through the long journey of this large group, the Chinese were looking for them. Both the weather and the terrain helped the Dalai Lama and his large entourage to escape undetected.

The 14th Dalai Lama, Tenzin Gyatso, entered Arunachal Pradesh on 31 March 1959 and took refuge at the Tawang monastery. I was already in Bom Dila to cover his arrival. In early April, the Dalai Lama arrived at the foothills of NEFA (North-East Frontier Agency) now Arunachal Pradesh. From there, he was escorted by train to Mussoorie. The Dalai Lama and Tibet's government-in-exile are now based in Dharamshala.

Indo-Chinese relations got steadily worse as the

Communist Government in Beijing was by now well settled by 1959. It no longer needed India's help. India had already made China a member of the Non-Aligned nations group. India now decided to assert its right to the international border. When India began patrolling Ladakh near the Tibet border, a police party was fired upon at Hot Springs on 21 October 1959. Nine policemen were killed, and others were taken prisoners. Their bodies were returned on Prime Minister Nehru's birthday, on 14 November—and of course it was a birthday which he did not celebrate.

Efforts were made thereafter to revive the deteriorating relations between the two countries. The Chinese were not only in possession of Aksai Chin but had moved considerably forward, laying claim to these areas. In the Northeast, they made claims even on the Arunachal province. India could not give up these areas and surrender before the aggressor. The Chinese had built up their military infrastructure and sent troops in large numbers to Tibet and other areas bordering India.

India's Defence Minister, V K Krishna Menon, had overlooked this situation despite the Army Chief's urgent reminders. Gen K S Thimayya, a highly decorated Chief of Army, resigned from this post in March 1959 when the Defence Minister refused to accept his report on the border situation with China. The Indian Army was still equipped with weapons from the Second World War and was not prepared to fight enemies armed with modern weapons. Krishna Menon had also failed to modernise the Indian Army. Strangely, when the whole world, including India's two inimical neighbours had embraced modern weapons, India's soldiers were still using outdated Enfield rifles and other vintage weapons. Krishna Menon was categorical in saying that China would never attack India. This was the strange state of India's Army while tension escalated with China.

Prime Minister Jawaharlal Nehru urged Gen Thimayya to withdraw his resignation, assuring him of taking action. Though Gen Thimayya withdrew his resignation, nothing was done. Krishna Menon, meanwhile, refused to accept recommendations for appointing a successor. He was clearly interfering with the norms of the defence forces, wanting to choose a successor of his own choice. This was bound to affect the army's morale.

India's relations with China, meanwhile, were getting worse. China was aware of the state of the Indian Army. Nehru wanted the Chinese to withdraw to the Line of Control as it existed before they moved into Aksai Chin. The Chinese refused, instead offering various solutions to diffuse the situation.

Sadly, Nehru's Intelligence Bureau chief, B M Mullick failed to provide him with accurate reports of the other side. I saw Mullick at work in 1961 during the liberation of Goa, where he acted almost as the Commander instead of Lt Gen J N Chaudhari who was officially in command. Moreover, Menon brought in his chosen officers, such as Lt Gen B M Kaul, who had never seen action in all his life. Why did the Prime Minister not stop his Defence Minister from doing all this? He had blindly trusted him far too much.

In Ladakh, a senseless forward-deployment policy had been adopted, to show India's flag at various points without the support of troops. No one realised that losing each post would later cost an area and ruin the nation's morale.

With no agreement in sight, the Chinese started moving forward and attacking. Asia's two largest countries were now at war. In a rush, India had to fly troops from Punjab, but when they arrived at the foothills of the NEFA region, there was no transport to take them further up. The troops had to march up the mountain towards Se La where India expected to stop the Chinese advance.

As a camera journalist covering the campaign, I found the artillery being positioned to support the infantry atop Se La, even as the jovial Punjab troops dug trenches. At a briefing, Gen Kaul addressed the media, but he seemed stuck in the strategies deployed during the First and Second World War. He had not anticipated that the Chinese may outflank the Indian positions and hit unexpectedly from behind. This is exactly what happened later.

The Chinese did exactly that. They attacked from behind and killed the troops marching up. Panic spread when the Chinese attacked unexpectedly. The government decided to vacate the areas on the North bank of the Brahmaputra River. Other journalists and I staying behind in Tezpur were asked to leave as the Indian command withdrew and the city was emptied. All around us, people were crying as they locked their homes and businesses and left. Even the prisoners from jail were released, and also the patients from mental asylums.

Pressurised by his party colleagues and people's protests, Nehru finally removed Krishna Menon from his job. I had decided to stay on in Tezpur, and so did another Indian journalist, B G Verghese. After reaching the foothills and the plains of Assam, the Chinese declared a unilateral ceasefire and started withdrawing to the McMahon line, which they had initially refused to accept. The war was over. India had been humiliated.

Nehru now had the hard task of reviving the Indian Army. Manpower and weaponry had to be increased considerably. The event left two major Asian nations in a state of undeclared war. By now, China had become increasingly interested in pulling other South Asian countries on its side.

Nehru then attempted to rebuild India's defence forces. During this time, I visited his home regularly and saw his health deteriorating, because of the partial stroke he had suffered around this time. While rebuilding the Indian Army, he also earnestly wanted to find a solution for Kashmir. He released his friend Sheikh Abdullah from jail, welcomed him home and asked him to travel to Pakistan to meet Ayub Khan. And just before he died, he had a long conversation with the Dalai Lama. He was known to be very fond of him. Nehru died on 27 May 1964, barely 20 months after the 1962 debacle. Lal Bahadur Shastri succeeded him.

Chapter 4

Afghanistan, an ancient land at the northern edge of the Indian subcontinent, has always been close to the heart of India. From the high mountains of the Hindukush, Afghanistan was once a part of the vast Mauryan Empire. It was from here that Emperor Kanishk sent Buddhist monks to China to spread the message of Buddhism. Afghanistan still has some of its ancient relics, even though it was unfortunate that the great Buddha statues of Bamiyan were destroyed by the Taliban, while they were functioning from Pakistan. The Afghans could do nothing to prevent this. It also ruined the tourism industry for the locals as thousands of tourists visited the area to see this wonder of the ancient world.

Afghanistan was a country where people once lived in peace despite belonging to different tribes. Hindus, Muslims and Sikhs—they were all one, though Muslims were always in the majority. Islam reached

India relatively late because Afghanistan, when it was a Hindu country, prevented seven Arab invasions meant to forcefully convert the inhabitants to Islam. Back then, the conversions to Islam were voluntary, as many lower-caste Hindus would find no caste discrimination in the enemy camp and preferred becoming Muslims. However, that is a different story.

Afghanistan has a rich history. It was through Afghanistan that Alexander reached India. Unable to proceed further into India after his victory over Porus, he turned back and stopped at Istalif, a hill resort north of Kabul. He eventually fell ill and died at Istalif, though there is a controversy whether his death occurred here or in Babylon. Afghanistan also finds mention in the great epic of Mahabharata; King Shakuni came from Gandhara, present-day Kandahar.

In 1751, Maharaja Ranjit of the Punjab Empire attacked Afghanistan to secure his domain. After defeating Ahmed Shah Durrani, Ranjit Singh restored him to his emirate but annexed the valley of Peshawar, including Peshawar city, which was Afghanistan's winter capital. The Khyber Pass and a large Pashtun area were also annexed. Those who take a keen interest in India's history would know that all invaders from the North, once they crossed the Khyber, could only be challenged in the plains of Panipat.

When Ranjit Singh passed away and the British

became India's new rulers, the Afghans sought their annexed territories back. Two Anglo-Afghan wars were fought, and the Punjab-Afghanistan border was restored with the dividing line being called the Durand Line. In recent times, Afghan ruler Mohammed Daud had asked Pakistan to return its territories, as had an earlier Taliban government. Afghanistan has not given up their claim on their territories.

Afghanistan was steadily progressing into the twentieth century under King Zahir Shah. He had cordial relations with the tribal chiefs whom he met and entertained every year and they supported all the reforms he introduced, like opening more schools and making education accessible to all. Kabul was a modern city in those days, and was constantly growing. It must be remembered that Afghans have always been clever businessmen. When the world did not even know how to deal in different currencies, Afghans were already doing so.

Jawaharlal Nehru visited Afghanistan in 1950. At the banquet in the Palace, the ladies of the royal family removed their veils and joined the gathering with the acknowledgement that India was their brother and so was Prime Minister Jawaharlal Nehru. There is no 'purdah', veil, between brothers and sisters. It was a successful visit that revived age-old brotherly relations between the two countries.

Afghanistan's transition from its ancient way of living

into modernity had made the country a tourist attraction. Back in the old days, a bus service operated between London and Calcutta, with a stopover in Kabul. Its success later led to another bus service between London and Delhi. This was possible because of peace in Iran, Afghanistan, and Pakistan, till it went under military rule in 1958 when Gen Ayub Khan took over.

In 1953, King Zahir Shah's first cousin, Mohammed Daud Khan, an ambitious person, persuaded King Zahir Shah and other religious leaders to make him the Prime Minister. Zahir Shah conceded to his request, which eventually had a tragic impact on Afghanistan's future.

King Zahir Shah had managed to keep Afghanistan away from the Cold War. He followed the Indian Non-Aligned policy despite being pressurised by both the US and the Soviet Union. Each wanted Afghanistan's support for their own reasons. The Soviets were looking for access to the warm waters of the Arabian Sea via the Baloch port at Gwadar. The US wanted Afghanistan on its side to stop the Soviets from advancing further into Central Asia.

Pakistan had joined the US-led military blocs SEATO (Southeast Asia Treaty Organization) and CENTO (Central Treaty Organization). Afghanistan was at peace with its steady progress and growth, and had remained non-aligned. Pakistan was able to use this ploy to get significant aid from the United States, which supported Pakistan with both funds and modern weapons.

To gain popularity, Mohammed Daud, Afghanistan's Prime Minister, urged Pakistan to return the former Afghan areas that continued to be occupied by Pakistan even after the British left. He also wholeheartedly supported the Pashtunistan movement led by Frontier Gandhi in Pakistan for a separate Pashtun country. Hence, Afghanistan's relations with Pakistan soon turned sour, affecting trade and business, including transit trade with India, as the supply of goods passed through Pakistan. Afghanistan gradually became more dependent on the Soviet Union for its needs.

The Soviet Union began inviting Afghan students on all-expenses-paid programmes. The students were given both accommodation and out-of-pocket expenses. For the Afghan students, the Soviet Union was a completely different world, and as several of them told me, it was like being in *jannat* or heaven. Afghanistan's army was already dependent on the Soviet Union for its training and arms supply. During a visit to some of the Afghan army commands, I felt as if it were an extension of the Soviet army.

King Zahir Shah decided to dismiss his Prime Minister as the country had deviated from the Non-Aligned Policy and was now completely dependent on the Soviet Union. After discussions with King Zahir Shah, Mohammed Daud resigned from the post of Prime Minister.

In June 1973, King Zahir Shah was in Italy with

his family for his medical treatment. Grabbing this opportunity and using his close personal ties with the Soviet Union and the Communist Party of Afghanistan, Mohammed Daud swung into action and staged a coup against his cousin, King Zahir Shah with the help of several army officers and the Communist Party of Afghanistan. The King was in no position to challenge him.

Mohammed Daud abolished the monarchy and the Parliamentary system and announced the establishment of the Republic of Afghanistan, appointing himself as President. He was now at the mercy of the Communist Party of Afghanistan and the Soviet Union as his support base to remain in power. This was the beginning of Afghanistan's troubles and eventual downfall.

Daud's earlier policy of sending students to the Soviet Union had resulted in a large number of government employees being either sympathetic to the Soviet Union or joining the Communist Party. Afghanistan was officially still following its Non-Aligned foreign policy, but it was increasingly being seen as a Soviet puppet.

Emperor Reza Shah Pahlavi was the all-powerful ruler of neighbouring Iran. It was also a Non-Aligned country, but close to the USA and its policies. Daud was in touch with the emperor, much to the displeasure of the Soviet Union. The Soviet Union did not approve of the Non-Aligned policy, particularly after Field Marshal Josip Broz

Tito of Yugoslavia successfully withdrew his country from the Soviet camp and became one of the pillars of the Non-aligned movement, together with Jawaharlal Nehru, President Sukarno of Indonesia and Gamal Abdel Nasser of Egypt, following their meeting in Belgrade, Yugoslavia.

Mohammed Daud proposed a meeting of the foreign Ministers of the Non-Aligned nations in Kabul in April 1979. The Soviets disapproved, seeing it as a repetition of the Belgrade meeting, after which Yugoslavia got out of the Soviet grouping of Communist East European Nations and joined the Western alliance under NATO.

As the day of the meeting neared, the Communist Party of Afghanistan (PDPA), with the support of the Afghan army, staged a coup against Mohammed Daud, killing him in the Presidential Palace along with his supporters and family members, including women and children. There was barely any public reaction because the Afghans disliked Daud for his treachery against King Zahir Shah.

Nur Muhammad Taraki, leader of the PDPA, was proclaimed to be the President of Afghanistan. At that time, I was in Kabul covering the aftermath of the coup and witnessed everything from the army tanks standing outside the Palace, and the victims in their blood-stained clothes, *et al.*

Taraki was a hard-core Communist leader who started by arresting people whose political ideology clashed with that of the communists. Unlike Mao, he did not kill millions, but several thousand were definitely killed all over Afghanistan. Divided as PDPA was between different factions, Taraki was killed by Hafizullah Amin on 19 September 1979. Hafizullah Amin, too, did not last long, as he was found to be even more cruel than Taraki. The Soviets suspected that he was also in touch with the Americans. He and his entire extended family were killed on 27 December 1979. The people of Afghanistan heaved a sigh of relief, but little did they know of what lay ahead.

The Soviet Union installed Babrak Karmal with a mandate to mend relations with the people. However, after successive coups and counter-coups, the Afghan army had lost its elan. Babrak Karmal requested the Soviet Union for help, and in no time, Soviet troops once again landed in Afghanistan with all their heavy weaponry. The people of Afghanistan considered it as an invasion by Soviet troops and were upset by their presence in their country.

At a large press conference in Kabul, attended by journalists and television crew from all over the world, Babrak Karmal tried to convince everyone that the Soviet troops were there only to stabilise the country and would leave soon. The hard-boiled media did not believe him and reports against the Babrak Karmal regime were soon out in the entire world. Finally, Karmal ordered the expulsion of most journalists from his country.

I decided to go to Ghazni, which is close to Kabul.

The people there were also angry about the arrival of the Soviet troops.

I visited the Indian Consulate office in Jalalabad. The situation was similar there. During my short stay in Jalalabad, I was able to call on Frontier Gandhi; he too spoke about the excesses of the Amin regime. As a firm believer of the Gandhian principle of non-violence, he felt that the solution to Afghanistan's problems lay in non-violence.

The tragedy of Afghanistan began soon after the arrival of Soviet troops. While the troops fanned out across the country to secure it, the US, along with Pakistan and Saudi Arabia, decided to intervene and fight them. This unfolded further tragic events that brought in major changes in Afghanistan, all of them serving to undo the steady progress Afghanistan had made under King Zahir Shah.

The axis of US, Pakistan and Saudi Arabia initially unleashed the Mujahideen against the Soviet troops. The Mujahideen soldiers were on a *jihad* against the so-called infidel regime of Babrak Karmal. However, most Mujahideen sold themselves to the Soviets and the Afghan government for money. This war began the exodus of the Afghans who could afford to move abroad, hoping for the situation to settle down before returning home.

When Pakistan and its allies realised that the war was not going in their favour, they recruited youngsters from

Pakistan and Afghan refugee camps, giving them a new name—the Taliban. They were to be fashioned into tough extremist Islamic fighters.

Afghanistan's economy now took a complete downturn. A fair number of its population had left the country for a safer refuge. A large population went to refugee camps in Pakistan, while most Hindus and Sikhs, made their way to India or to other countries.

With Babrak Karmal failing to bring peace to Afghanistan or to win the people's support, and with a new regime under Gorbachev coming to power in the Soviet Union in May 1986, it was again time for change in Afghanistan. Babrak Karmal made way for Mohammed Najibullah, whose first priority was to gain the confidence of the Afghan people. He renamed the Communist Party as Watan Party and began eradicating the vestiges of the Communist regime to make the country democratic again.

The war in Afghanistan had damaged the Soviet economy, in addition to heavy manpower losses. When Gorbachev came to power, he wanted to withdraw his forces from Afghanistan and found Najibullah in agreement with his wishes. Najibullah, whom I got to know well, believed that the Soviet withdrawal would win him the confidence of the people. This helped him win the Afghans' trust. He also won back the trust of tribal leaders by giving them the respect due to them.

Najibullah was shocked to find the state of the Afghan

army. The presence of the Soviet army had reduced the Afghan army to a secondary force. Najibullah, with the help of other senior officers, now began rebuilding the force.

In the country's north, Ahmad Shah Massoud, a nationalist leader, was in control of Panjshir and surrounding areas during the Communist rule. He welcomed Najib's plans and, on hearing of Pakistan's plans to attack Kabul, marched to the capital.

Meanwhile, news from the Soviet Union was not good. It soon began to disintegrate under Gorbachev. A coup against him led both to his resignation and the rise of Yeltsin, who completed the disintegration of the Soviet Union. The Soviet flag was lowered and the Russian flag was raised in its place. Thus ended the great Communist revolution of the Soviet Union. Yeltsin stopped arms assistance to Afghanistan. Najibullah soon found himself bereft of Soviet support prompting him to resign and take shelter in the UN compound in Afghanistan.

Meanwhile, India took steps to bring Najibullah and his family to Delhi, but they were stopped at the airport by the men of warlord Gen Dostum, who also facilitated the Taliban's march towards Kabul after he withdrew his forces from the border with Pakistan. This treacherous act ultimately resulted in the Taliban entering Kabul and dragging Najibullah and his brother out of the United Nations compound, where they were brutally killed.

What followed was a long and tragic story, with

America directly entering the Afghan war to defeat the Taliban. After successfully removing the first Taliban government and fighting for almost twenty years, America withdrew abruptly, restoring the Taliban to power again. Twenty years of rebuilding Afghanistan were blown up in a minute when President Biden ordered the withdrawal of US troops. The unplanned withdrawal literally amounted to an escape from Afghanistan.

Afghanistan has since surrendered to the Taliban following President Biden's decision. Women have been the worst sufferers, being denied education, and jobs. Though currently India does not have an Embassy in Kabul, it maintains its relationship with the current regime. Only time will tell whether Afghanistan can ever return to being the modern nation that it was more than fifty years ago under King Zahir Shah. This South Asian country has suffered a sea change since then.

Amidst all this, Pakistan plans to continue the fighting in Afghanistan. After the loss of East Pakistan, it had sought to increase its depth, and has found a perfect opportunity now, at a time when Russia had also stopped its aid to Afghanistan. Afghanistan's tragedy thus continues. Pakistan seemingly succeeded in installing a government in Kabul sympathetic to it, but this did not work in their favour either.

It is now apparent that the new Taliban government in Kabul is not sympathetic towards Pakistan. There have been several clashes along the Durand line, where Pakistan was creating a barbed-wire wall. Several Pakistan army soldiers have died in these clashes. The current Taliban government in Afghanistan has refused to accept this border or relinquish its claims over territories annexed by Ranjit Singh centuries ago.

Chapter 5

Army-controlled Pakistan has nevertheless kept up a facade of holding elections to form a new government and members of Assembly every five years, pretending as if the army was never its real ruling power. Governments elected this way do not even last a full term, surviving only as long as they do not have a difference of opinion with the army. The last elected and very popular Prime Minister, Imran Khan, is in jail despite anger and agitation across the country about his imprisonment.

The December 1970 election was a watershed moment in Pakistan's history. The Awami League, led by Sheikh Mujibur Rahman, made an all-out effort to win the elections. During the election campaign, Sheikh Mujib declared that his government would work for the upliftment of the poor in Pakistan, and that the army belonged in the barracks. Leaders in West Pakistan, particularly Zulfikar Ali Bhutto of the Pakistan Peoples

Party, were sure of their win and usually, it was leaders or parties from West Pakistan that ruled the roost because votes in East Pakistan were often divided.

The 1971 elections were hotly contested and resulted in the victory of the Awami League. It secured 167 seats in the National Assembly out of a total of 313 seats. This meant that Sheikh Mujib would be the next Prime Minister of Pakistan. The Awami league also won 288 seats out of 300 in the Provincial Assembly of East Pakistan. The elections had given a clear mandate to the Awami League leader Sheikh Mujibur Rahman.

The result was unacceptable to President Gen Yahya Khan. Zulfikar Ali Bhutto, who hoped to become the next Prime Minister of Pakistan, was also shocked and refused to accept the result. The President took no steps to invite Sheikh Mujib to form the government. Bhutto offered convoluted solutions for the impasse, such as appointing two Prime Ministers for Pakistan, which Sheikh Mujib rightly rejected.

Two months passed after the election results were out, and the President had taken no step to invite the leader of the majority party to form the government. The army clearly did not wish a Bengali to be the President. For the West Pakistan region and the army, East Pakistan was more like a colony, rather than a part of Pakistan.

On 15 March, Gen Yahya Khan flew to Dhaka to resolve the issue. Bhutto was present for the meeting.

The proposal for two Prime Ministers was rejected by Sheikh Mujib. The talks failed and the General flew back to Islamabad. Addressing a public rally, Sheikh Mujib declared that any further agitation now would be for the liberation of Bengal. Meanwhile, Gen Yahya Khan appointed Gen Tikka Khan as the new Governor for East Pakistan. After giving a deadline of 25 March to the President, Sheikh Mujib declared that East Pakistan no longer existed and that Bangladesh was now a sovereign, independent country. This was officially confirmed on 26 March 1971 at Chittagong. The die was cast.

Gen Tikka Khan, whom the Bengali judges of East Pakistan (now Bangladesh), had refused to swear in as Governor of the province, declared a state of emergency and cracked down on the people of East Pakistan with a heavy hand by imposing martial law. He had already strengthened the presence of Punjabi soldiers from West Pakistan in the province. Moreover, he ordered the presence of Razakars, a paramilitary force made up of extremist, Urdu-speaking, anti-Bengali people. This group largely comprised of immigrants from Bihar in India. A wave of merciless killings of Awami League supporters was unleashed. In an attack on the Dhaka University hostel, students who had not yet left for their homes were lined up and shot dead.

Sheikh Mujibur Rahman was arrested, flown to West Pakistan and imprisoned. In other parts of East

Pakistan, the army was ordered to curb the agitation and kill the protestors. By then, I had arrived in Calcutta to cover events in East Pakistan, and together with a colleague, the late Durgadas Chatterji, I drove down to the Benapole border. We had hoped to find it open, but it was not and it was being patrolled by Pakistani border guards and immigration officials. We were told that an agitation against Pakistan had also erupted in Jessore. The road from Benapole led to Jessore, where there was a Pakistan army cantonment.

Three days later, the border guards and immigration officials at the border had disappeared. The Indian side told us that the guards and other officials on the other side feared being killed by protestors. There were reports that several people had already been killed by the army on the outskirts of Jessore.

We decided to take the risk and crossed over to see what was going on in Jessore. Reaching the outskirts of Jessore, we were shocked to see a large number of dead bodies strewn around. Our driver told us that they had been killed by the army the previous day for demonstrating against the regime in West Pakistan.

We moved to the railway station, which was virtually closed, with no signs of routine activity. The city was shut, fearing more army killings. It was clear to both of us that the agitation for Bangladesh that began on 25 March had now spread into the interiors of the country. The army's crackdown on the population was merciless. All the army units in action were from West Pakistan's Punjab or Baloch regions. The few Bengali units of the Pakistan army that existed were either in West Pakistan or confined to their barracks.

The genocidal killings ordered by Gen Tikka Khan were more than a crackdown to restore law and order in the country. It had turned into a civil war between unarmed native people of East Pakistan and the heavily armed West Pakistanis. In addition, thousands of families began heading for India.

India now had a huge problem on its hands—looking after these migrants in camps set up near the border to stop them from further entering into the country.

The world also began to take notice of this. Journalists were not allowed into East Pakistan. They were based largely in Calcutta, covering the misery of people from East Pakistan now living in camps set up by India. The number of people entering India continued to rise, crossing a million and rising further. There were Hindus, Muslims, and Buddhists—people of all religions from East Pakistan. At one point, it seemed that Gen Tikka Khan and his soldiers were targeting only the Hindus. Thousands of women, both Muslim and Hindu, were kidnapped and raped by soldiers of the Pakistan army. It was the worst kind of atrocity that anyone in the world could suffer.

Young Bangladeshis soon organised themselves and

received military training with India's help. The Mukti Bahini emerged from among the refugees, as well as from inhabitants in Chittagong and other areas. Pakistan's Bengal regiments based in East Pakistan also rebelled, as the families of several Bengali soldiers had suffered atrocities while their men served in West Pakistan. Many such families had to flee to India to escape the West Pakistani Punjabi soldiers who were now ruling East Pakistan.

India appealed to the world and to the Human Rights Organization to take note of the plight of people of East Pakistan. The USA was then ruled by President Nixon who was hostile to India's Prime Minister, Indira Gandhi. She undertook a tour to several nations to personally apprise them of the situation and the heavy expense and responsibility that India was bearing in its humane effort in looking after the refugees. She also went to Washington to apprise President Nixon, who met her but did nothing to stop the Pakistan government's actions in East Pakistan.

India concluded that it would have to manage the escalating situation on its own. It was now clear that the people of East Pakistan would not give up their demand for Bangladesh, having already formed a provisional government in exile. For the Bengalis of East Pakistan, it was no longer about Mujib's prime ministership; they were now demanding their own country—Bangladesh.

On entering Chuadanga, which had been declared the provisional capital of the Bangladesh government, I found the city awash with flags of the Awami League and under the control of an Awami League leader popularly known as Two Gun Haq—the man who carried two guns and went around town. The Pakistan army had not yet reached there. Later, the town also fell into the hands of the Pakistan army and Haq's rule did not last long. Like most other Awami League leaders and the people of East Pakistan, he too escaped to India seeking refuge.

Instead of resolving the issue in East Pakistan and accepting the election results, Pakistan continued its crackdown in East Pakistan. It also began planning to attack India in the north to stop Indian support to the Mukti Bahini and the Bangladesh government-in-exile. India had not yet recognised the provisional government of Bangladesh announced by the Awami League leaders.

Meanwhile, in July 1971, Pakistan had helped US National Security Advisor Henry Kissinger to fly to Beijing from Islamabad, taking the world by surprise.

It was clear that the US under President Nixon was going to recognise Communist China, dropping their age-old ally—the Chiang Kai-shek-led Kuomintang regime in Formosa—since they were unable to regain control of Communist China and move back to the mainland. Pakistan's offer of help cemented their relationship with both the US and China. With Kissinger's successful visit to China, Nixon announced that he would visit People's Republic of China, now under Mao in the coming year.

When Indira Gandhi toured the western capitals to explain the situation in East Pakistan and the plight of India currently burdened with refugees, she began her meetings by first visiting the US to meet President Nixon. Mrs Gandhi found Nixon utterly unsympathetic and it was clear to her that he was not going to upset Pakistan's President, who had earlier helped Kissinger travel to China. It must be noted that this action marked the beginning of Pakistan's special and close relationship with the US and China. For India, the US has never been a reliable friend.

Earlier, in September, Mrs Gandhi had visited the Soviet Union to meet President Brezhnev and Prime Minister Kosygin. They were clearly sympathetic to India, and agreed that the only solution to the problem would be military action. Pakistan would not take back the millions of people it had pushed into India. She was assured of military aid from the Soviet Union if required. This assurance capped the Treaty of friendship that India had signed earlier with the Soviet Union.

Pakistan felt bolstered when the US did not entertain Mrs Gandhi. Their President had already planned to keep Indian forces away from East Pakistan. Gen Yahya Khan ordered his air force to attack India on 3 December 1971. Seeing Pakistan's aggression, India fought back. Indira Gandhi was in Calcutta then, addressing the people of Bengal, explaining that though the world was sympathetic towards India, no one had done anything to help.

After returning to Delhi, Mrs Gandhi held an emergency meeting of the cabinet and met the Opposition leaders, who assured her of full support.

Thereafter, India's response was quick and lethal for Pakistan. Gen Sam Manekshaw had prepared the forces well, and Indian troops quickly moved into East Pakistan. On 6 December 1971, India officially recognised Bangladesh in Parliament. East Pakistan was gone—a new country had emerged in South Asia.

To help Pakistan, President Nixon ordered the nuclear-powered Seventh Fleet into the Bay of Bengal. Indian forces were, by then, outflanking Pakistan forces and had advanced towards Dhaka. India's navy and its aircraft carrier were in action, too. The Soviet Union ordered one of its naval fleets to trail the Seventh fleet of the US. President Nixon alleged that India was getting aggressive in the war, forgetting that it was Pakistan that had initiated attack on 3 December. India's counter-attack began on 4 December, pushing the Pakistan army back. It is a known fact that the Pakistan army commanders in East Pakistan were waiting for the US army or the air force to support them.

On 9 December, Gen Manekshaw called upon Pakistan forces to surrender, assuring them protection as per military rules. The Eastern Command of India under Lt Gen J S Arora was ready. After negotiations with

Pakistan's commander in East Pakistan, Gen Lt Niazi, and Maj Gen Jacob of the Indian Army flew into Dhaka on 16 December with a draft of the Surrender document.

The surrender ceremony took place on the same day at the Race Course grounds where Lt Gen Niazi, commander of Pakistan's forces in East Pakistan, formally surrendered by placing his revolver on the table. The representative of the Provisional Government of Bangladesh was also present. This was the biggest surrender in world history, with 93,000 Pakistani soldiers surrendering. They were allowed to carry their weapons till they entered their cantonments where they handed over their weapons to the Indian Army.

The Provisional Government of Bangladesh flew in from Calcutta the next day and took charge of the country. At this stage, the government of Bangladesh was headed by Tajuddin Ahmed. It was not easy to bring stability to the country as the Bengali population was wanting to harm the Urdu-speaking community that had migrated to East Pakistan during the Partition. Their businesses were looted; they were ousted from their homes. I witnessed even small Urdu-speaking vendors ending up in refugee camps. Bangladesh wanted them to return to Pakistan. Over half a million of them were in various camps. Many managed to escape in the chaos following the victory of the Indian Army.

Sheikh Mujibur Rahman was still in jail in Rawalpindi. After negotiations, in which the UK also intervened, he was freed and allowed to travel to London. The Pakistan government did not allow him to go via India. From London, he flew to Delhi, where Indira Gandhi congratulated him. He then flew to Dhaka on 10 January 1972. It was a huge welcome and I had occasion to cover it. It took several hours for him to travel in a procession to address a rally where people from all over Bangladesh had come.

Sheikh Mujib was sworn in as President of the new country of Bangladesh. Later, when the Constitution was finalised, he became the Prime Minister of a Parliamentary democracy. Running a new country with no resources and a treasury emptied by Pakistan, was not easy and the government of the newly independent country had to start afresh. However, Sheikh Mujib was a nationalist and followed socialist economic policies. The Constitution had proclaimed Bangladesh to be secular. These were opposed by extremist Islamic elements and those belonging to the former Muslim League who were dissatisfied with the recent happenings.

Sheikh Mujib also followed an independent foreign policy, maintaining close friendship with India and its Prime Minister, Indira Gandhi. Soon there was unrest in the country as prices rose along with rampant corruption. Instead of finding a solution, Sheikh Mujib tried to bring the country under one-party rule, as often happened in Communist countries. He forgot that there were considerable votes against him despite winning majority seats in the 1971 Pakistan election.

On 15 August 1975, several army officers, with Khondaker Mostaq Ahmad in the forefront, staged a coup against Sheikh Mujib, and killed him and his family. His daughter, Hasina escaped because she was abroad, where her husband was working. Thus, ended the short-term rule of Sheikh Mujib, during which the country also suffered a famine.

Bangladesh has not stabilised since. Sheikh Hasina, Sheikh Mujib's daughter eventually returned to Bangladesh and became its Prime Minister from 1996 to 2001. She lost the 2001 election, but was reelected in 2009, and then served for four successive terms. During this period, she managed to bring some prosperity to her country. Bangladesh took the lead in garments exports. However, each of her victories in elections, including the 2024 elections, were marred by serious charges of rigging. She fought the charges and even brought in a law seeking job reservations for the descendants of freedom fighters. A massive student-led agitation followed, which resulted in her fleeing to India.

Mohammed Yunus came from the US to take charge of the country amidst the chaos. The country continues to live in turmoil, with charges and counter-charges over whether a US-Pakistan conspiracy led to the downfall of Sheikh Hasina.

The agonising part is that a country strategically located in the Bay of Bengal may also become a victim of global power play, as happened to Afghanistan.

Chapter 6

Lal Bahadur Shastri succeeded Prime Minister Nehru as India's Prime Minister. The 1960s had been a difficult time for India, with the country facing many challenges. There was not enough food to keep its population fed; wheat and rice were major imports. The Fabian socialist policies adopted by the government had pushed up prices of essential commodities. High taxation rates had resulted in money leaving India, as wealthy Indians opened their accounts abroad and moved their money there. There was income tax, along with wealth tax and sales tax that burdened people. Sales tax pinched both retailers and shoppers, and affected the rich and the poor. Shastri took charge of a country whose people were unhappy, and assured them of improving the situation.

For Gen Ayub Khan, it was the right opportunity to attempt to capture Kashmir. Former Prime Minister Jawaharlal Nehru had used all his diplomatic skills to prevent Pakistan from attacking India after the setback suffered by the Indian Army against the Chinese. Gen Ayub Khan took India by surprise when he sent his troops into the Rann of Kutch in western India, near Karachi. There had been some difference of opinion about the border drawn by Radcliffe at the time of the Partition. The disputed border gave him the pretext for aggression.

The Rann of Kutch is a marshy area, home to wild asses. India had only a few border posts in the area and very limited military presence. Gen Ayub Khan moved an infantry division supported by armoured regiments. Little did he realise that India's response could be strong, and that it was no longer what it was in 1962. Since then, Nehru had worked relentlessly to modernise and rebuild the army.

India gave a tough response, beating back the Patton tanks given to Pakistan by the US. Pakistan suffered heavy casualties. Ayub's army was not supposed to use the Patton tanks and other military weapons supplied by the US against India. And all this while India had repeatedly warned the US that the arms provided to Pakistan would be eventually used against India. This is exactly what happened.

India's response to Pakistan's Operation Desert Hawk in the Rann of Kutch left Gen Ayub Khan in total shock. India had not moved any troops or equipment from the North and only the local command in the area handled the situation. Eventually, Anglo-American powers intervened to rescue Pakistan from its failed offensive. Finally, a UN-mediated ceasefire came into effect on 1 July 1965. Both India and Pakistan agreed to settle the dispute of the area through the International Court of Justice.

To overcome the embarrassment of the defeat over Rann of Kutch, Gen Ayub Khan initiated Operation Gibraltar in Kashmir. Pakistan sent in troops in civil dress, posing as locals, thus having well-trained men from the Pakistan army infiltrate Kashmir, seeking local support and bringing about an uprising.

Operation Gibraltar depended upon the support of local Kashmiris. It failed as Kashmiris hate Punjabi Muslims. They willingly set off to inform the authorities of the infiltrators' presence. With no cooperation from the locals, the infiltrators began sabotage in the area, such as cutting telephone lines, and blowing up electrical transmission towers.

When I arrived in Srinagar to cover this insurgence, my taxi got hit by a bullet as we drove from the airport towards the hotel. The taxi driver commented, 'the bastards are roaming nearby', and explained about the infiltrators. By then, India was aware that infiltration into Jammu and Kashmir was on a large scale, involving enough soldiers that would have comprised a complete division. Prime Minister Shastri chose to confront the enemy directly instead of merely arresting and pushing them back.

The Indian Army decided to attack Haji Pir Pass and

stop any further infiltration. I climbed up to the top of Haji Pir and slept in an area under the Indian Artillery forces as it began pounding Pak positions. Gen Ayub Khan was taken by surprise. All efforts by the Pakistan army to recapture the strategic Haji Pir, thereby, failed.

Pakistan moved more troops to cut India's land route to Kashmir by attacking the Chicken's neck area near Jammu. For the first time, Indian forces crossed into Pakistan. The war went beyond Jammu and Kashmir, as the Indian Army fast advanced towards Lahore and Sialkot.

Pakistan used US-provided Sabre jets, but Indian Gnats, with well-trained pilots, took them on and shot them down, much to the shock of the US as well. I was covering what was said to have been the biggest tank battle since the Second World War. Indian tanks and army had reached the outskirts of Sialkot, a city famous for producing and exporting sports goods, where the tank battle was raging.

Maj Gen Rajinder Singh 'Sparrow', the commander of the Indian Armoured Division, escorted the press party himself in a tank. As the press party moved on, four Sabre jets of the Pakistan Air Force suddenly appeared in the sky. We were in the open and dashed down into bunkers. Over the next twenty or twenty-five minutes, the four Sabres failed to hit even a single tank. Everyone heaved a sigh of relief. Maj Gen 'Sparrow's' ADC, who was in a jeep parked under a tree, was hit in the leg. This reflects on the capability of the so-called 'superior' Pakistan Air Force, which failed even to hit sitting targets.

Another instance when India took the enemy by surprise was when its forces reached the outskirts of Pakistan's largest city of Lahore, the capital of Punjab. India decided not to capture the city, even as large numbers of local people began leaving for Rawalpindi. Gen Ayub Khan's Operation Gibraltar and Operation Grand Slam had both failed. The little man from New Delhi—Prime Minister Shastri so called because his height was only 5 feet 2 inches—had won against the tall, robust General from Rawalpindi.

Pakistan had planned to give a befitting reply to India's move into Sialkot and Lahore in heavy Patton tanks with which they hoped to capture Indian territory up to the Beas River. This came to be known as the Battle of Asal Uttar where Maj Gen Gurbaksh Singh, commander of Indian Infantry forces in Punjab, decided to destroy the heavy US Patton tanks. He used water from the nearby canals and flooded the agricultural fields from where Pakistan's heavy Patton tanks were to go. The Indian General had surrounded the area with his World War 2 Sherman and Centurion tanks positioned in a horseshoe shape. As expected, when the Patton tanks tried to drive through the fields, they were bogged down by the muddy fields. The tanks and Pakistani forces were now sitting targets for India to shoot down.

The world took instant note, particularly the US, Pakistan's mentor and supplier of weapons. They now wanted to save Pakistan from complete humiliation. After heavy casualties on both sides, the UN declared a ceasefire on 23 September, exactly 23 days after Pakistan had started Operation Grand Slam. The battle of Asal Uttar was a heavy defeat for Pakistan, when Gen Ayub's dream of capturing Amritsar lay stuck in muddy fields. India's army had retrieved its reputation damaged in the 1962 fight against the Chinese.

It was also the first time that India had crossed its borders to attack another country. The powerful dynasties of South India—the Cholas, Chalukyas, Pallavas and others, had strong naval strength. When they moved towards Southeast Asia, they had gone with positive intent, and never with the aim of conquering another nation. They went to construct great Hindu temples in countries like Cambodia, Vietnam, Sumatra, and Indonesia among others.

Prime Minister Shastri had declared that India was tired of sending infiltrators back into Pakistan. It was time for action, just as the recent retaliation ordered by Prime Minister Modi under Operation Sindoor was forced upon India due to cross-border terrorism.

Shastri's success against Gen Ayub Khan proved him to be a decisive and powerful leader. His colleagues in the Congress Party now looked at him with respect. He also voiced his ideas of reviving the Indian economy that had suffered as a result of several Fabian Socialist policies and announced that he would work on rationalising high taxation rates that had driven businessmen and industrialists to park their profits and money in banks outside India.

With Indian forces now positioned on the outskirts of Lahore, Sialkot and in many areas of occupied Kashmir, including the strategic Haji Pir Pass, Gen Ayub became a target of his enemies in Pakistan. India ignored America's requests to resume negotiations with Pakistan. In my opinion, the Soviet Union now suddenly saw an opportunity to intervene. India was already largely dependent upon the Soviet Union for purchasing arms and had friendly relations with them.

India, however, agreed to meet Pakistan in Tashkent, the capital of Uzbekistan, in extreme winter.

When the negotiations began, India was pressurised to give up all the captured areas. As far as I know, India agreed for withdrawal from the mainland Pakistani areas, but refused to withdraw from Pakistan-occupied Kashmir, as Kashmir is an integral part of India.

On 10 January, the Indian media were told that the talks had failed and they could freely go into the city. Suddenly, Soviet officials turned up, announcing that a compromise had been reached and a Declaration was going to be signed. This took everyone by surprise. As the Tashkent Declaration was signed, it became clear that status quo ante had been restored to Pakistan's advantage. The Declaration was signed despite the Indian Army's objections to the return of captured areas.

In my opinion, the Soviet Union had its own advantage in enforcing such a document on India. Perhaps it hoped to influence Pakistan to opt out of the US alignment.

On the night of signing the Tashkent Declaration, I and the late N S Thapa of the Government of India's Films Division went to meet Prime Minister Shastri, who was still working on some papers.

Later that night, a Soviet official informed, 'Your Prime Minister has died. Please come downstairs'.

Lal Bahadur Shastri passed away on 11 January 1966. It was informed that he seemed to have had a massive heart attack, and while looking for medical assistance, he had died in the arms of the Soviet Guard.

Indian media waited outside in freezing weather for hours before being taken to the airport. Prime Minister Shastri's cortege arrived with dignitaries, including Gen Ayub Khan. What should have been a satisfying moment after the Declaration had turned into one of sorrow.

India suffered a double shock—the death of Shastri and the signing of the declaration that condoned Pakistan's aggression besides surrendering areas that were legitimately India's.

G L Nanda, a senior minister in the late PM Shastri's

cabinet, took over as the interim Prime Minister while the Congress Party decided on a successor. After much deliberation, the name decided upon was Mrs Indira Gandhi's, who had been the Information Minister in the Shastri cabinet. Morarji Desai contested against her when the Parliamentary Party of the Congress Party met to elect its leader. Later, Mrs Indira Gandhi won the 1967 election for the Congress Party and became Prime Minister.

She took charge of India at a time when her predecessor Shastri was working on the state of India's economy and the food shortage. Bihar was facing famine with a severe drought. After much negotiations, India imported food grains from the US, paying in Indian rupees under a scheme known as the PL 480. Under this scheme, the US could use the accumulated rupees for their expenses in India on their Embassy, Consulates, and other offices.

I travelled from Delhi to Bihar to see the ground realities for myself. Never had I seen fertile soil so cracked up. Some farmers were even using buckets of water to moisten the soil. India had seen forty-three famines during the British era. Indira Gandhi not only fought what could have been a severe famine—she also ensured that no one died of hunger.

Despite a challenging start to her tenure, Gandhi met them head-on and successfully. Soon she took on the economy and the problems of the rupee. The official exchange rate for the rupee at that time was Rs 4.70 to a dollar, but the market rate was Rs 10 or even more to a dollar. Mrs Indira Gandhi took the bold step of devaluing the rupee.

Moreover, she later nationalised fourteen leading banks of India. She also reduced the majority control of foreign investors in Indian companies. When the then Prime Minister Jawaharlal Nehru was asked why he allowed foreign companies to retain a majority, his reply had been that there was no point in wasting money on nationalising firms working under Indian laws. He instead, preferred using the money to build new companies. This eventually became a policy and a principle.

Senior Congress Party leaders who had expected to control government policies under Indira Gandhi suddenly felt sidelined. That is a different story. Everyone was now of the opinion that the Prime Minster was strong, and had her own mind and policies. When I interviewed her, Mrs Gandhi described India's Parliamentary democracy as moribund. She floated the idea of introducing the presidential system but it was as quickly dropped as it was floated. India continued as a parliamentary democracy.

Chapter 7

Mrs Indira Gandhi had settled down as the Prime Minister by the end of 1970 and had entered the new year with renewed confidence. She was no longer dependent on the old guard of the Congress, who were gone after the Party split. She was now the leader of the Indian National Congress (R). Being confident that the people of India had accepted her leadership, she decided it was time to call for a General Election for the Lok Sabha. She neither sought nor took support from the parties that had kept her government afloat after the Congress had split.

The General elections to elect 518 members of the Lok Sabha were held in March 1971. To her surprise, this election gave her a landslide victory, giving her 352 seats out of 518. The old Indian National Congress, which was a threat to her government after the split, was nearly wiped out, winning only sixteen seats. The Bharatiya Jana Sangh, the predecessor of the BJP, managed an impressive twenty-two seats. The remaining seats went to other regional parties, including the two Communist parties. Mrs Gandhi had emerged as a powerful leader of India.

Across the border, President Gen Yahya Khan had held elections to the National Assembly in December 1970. In Pakistan, where the military has continued to rule since the coup by Gen Ayub Khan, elections were held merely to give legitimacy to military rule. The elected government would toe the line set by the President, that is, the army. The majority of East Pakistan had 162 seats because of its large population, while West Pakistan had 138. West Pakistan would invariably win because of the divided East Pakistan parties. However, in the 1970 elections, the Awami League was led by a powerful leader, Sheikh Mujibur Rahman, who took advantage of people's resentment over the language crises and the forced imposition of Urdu in East Pakistan.

The 1970 elections in Pakistan were bitter. Sheikh Mujibur defended not only the Bengali language but also declared that the army belonged in its barracks. On the other hand, the Pakistan Peoples Party led by Zulfikar Ali Bhutto, faced tough opposition from other Islamist parties, including the Muslim League. Bhutto, from Sindh, was not acceptable to the Punjabis, Balochis, and people from the NWFP. With all the divisions, the election results were predicted to go in favour of East Pakistan's Sheikh Mujib.

When the results were announced, it was clear that

the next Prime Minister of Pakistan would be Sheikh Mujibur Rahman and this was unacceptable to Gen Yahya Khan and Zulfikar Ali Bhutto in West Pakistan. A stalemate followed. Bhutto suggested having two Prime Ministers for Pakistan, although it was not proposed in the Constitution of Pakistan nor did such a system ever exist in Parliamentary democracies anywhere. The Parliament can have only one Prime Minister and a leader of the Opposition, a role unacceptable to Bhutto.

Gen Yahya Khan nominated Nurul Amin, a retired Bengali leader, as Prime Minister, asking him to bring about a compromise between Mujibur and Bhutto. This delay was causing unrest in East Pakistan, yet Gen Yahya Khan did not invite Mujibur Rahman to form the government.

Instead of honouring and accepting the election results, Gen Yahya Khan launched a military operation called 'Operation Searchlight' in East Pakistan. Its primary aim was to unleash civil war in the region. Sheikh Mujibur Rahman had already made it clear to people in both East and West Pakistan that any agitation now would be to get independence for the creation of Bangladesh. Gen Yahya Khan overlooked this warning.

Addressing a mass rally in Dhaka on 7 March 1971, more than three months after the election results, Sheikh Mujibur declared, '*Ae baar sangram, mukti sangram*'—the struggle this time will be a liberation struggle. He knew that the people of East Pakistan would no longer tolerate the high-handedness of the Punjabi-dominated Pakistan army. In his speech, Mujibur gave the rulers in Rawalpindi a deadline of 25 March to honour the election result.

In response, Yahya Khan sent Gen Tikka Khan with orders to crush the agitation in East Pakistan. Gen Tikka Khan cracked down on the people of East Pakistan as reinforcements had been flown from West Pakistan. Sheikh Mujibur Rahman was arrested and flown to Rawalpindi. Meanwhile, in Dhaka, the Bengali judges refused to swear in Gen Tikka Khan as Governor of East Pakistan.

I had already reached Calcutta, wondering how to cover the situation in East Pakistan. Gen Tikka Khan had already ordered all foreign correspondents to leave Dhaka so that the world would not know what was happening in East Pakistan. After the proclamation of Bangladesh, Awami League leaders and those of other political parties had either sought refuge in Calcutta or had gone underground to escape the crackdown.

It was a time of terror in East Pakistan. Students in Dhaka hostels had been lined up in open spaces and shot down. House-to-house searches followed to trace more 'trouble makers'. Women were kidnapped and raped. To save their lives and families, people, particularly the Hindus, had started moving towards India to seek refuge in refugee camps opened by the Indian government to prevent people from joining the local Bengali population.

Protests filed to Pakistan went unanswered. The world simply watched, as Pakistan was a close ally of the Western Military alliances and almost a protectorate of the USA.

This author, then representing Visnews, the world's biggest TV News Agency, would go to the Benapole border post each day hoping to legally enter Pakistan. It would always be a waste of time. There was no point in entering through an unprotected border area as that would mean being on foot. But as mentioned in an earlier chapter, we were soon able to enter East Pakistan when we found the Benapole Border post deserted and unmanned after a few days. My colleague and I just walked in.

We were lucky to find a vehicle whose owner offered to take us halfway through to Jessore. This sounded great to both of us and the car owner dropped us at a restaurant that had a small crowd inside. They were all listening to the news from All India Radio. We were reassured that the crowd wouldn't be hostile. We had taken the risk of entering East Pakistan knowing the consequences. No other journalist, including the foreign journalists, had taken such a step. A gentleman at the restaurant offered to take us to Jessore and show us what had happened the previous day.

On the outskirts of the city of Jessore, we found a road turning left which had a strong barricade marked No Entry. The road led to the army cantonment. We stopped here to film the large number of dead bodies lying there from the firing on these demonstrators the previous day. We requested our local host to take us to the railway station. I was hoping to establish the location of the incident of this gruesome killing by showing the nearest railway station. From there, we were again lucky to find a small group of protestors who offered to take us back to the border.

Thanking the kind car owner who had brought us to Jessore, both myself and Durgadas Chatterji got into the jeep that was to take us back to the border. However, the agitators first took us to a place where they had gathered several Urdu-speaking Pakistanis. It was clear to us that these poor souls were soon going to be killed. I requested the jeep owner to take us back as it was time we got back to India. I can never forget the speed with which those guys drove us back to Benapole. All through it seemed that the jeep could meet with an accident any moment. We arrived at Benapole safely and crossing back into India, we both touched the soil and thanked the Lord for protecting us.

Indian border guards congratulated us on our safe return. There was an army officer who had travelled from Fort William in Calcutta with us and was waiting for us to return. He wanted to know what we had seen. First he thought that we were pulling a fast one, but when I explained the location of the trijunction and the barricade, he looked at us in awe. He said that was the barricade put up by the Pakistan army who must have been under orders not to fire as they had done the previous day. This was the first visual evidence that the world would see in countries like the United States of America and Europe, countries that were allies of Pakistan. How could Pakistan now deny that there were no killings in East Pakistan.

Getting back to Calcutta, our first task was to file a news report for Reuters news agency that was associated with Visnews. Our next task was to advise the Chief Editor of Visnews of what we had shot. His advice after thanking us for all the risks we had taken, was: 'Don't do it again.' This kind of advice was the norm, but if I had not taken the risk, then how else was I to report or show what was happening in East Pakistan?

The number of people fleeing East Pakistan continued to rise, crossing over a million. The miserable refugees were looted by the Pakistani police as they walked towards India. In the villages, Pakistani police and army kidnapped and raped women, besides looting their homes and killing the menfolk.

I and my colleague Durgadas Chatterji had also entered Chuadanga, as I mentioned before in an earlier chapter, the provisional capital of Bangladesh which was like a small town. The local Awami League leader, Dr Ashdul Haq had taken charge of the city, throwing out its Pakistani administrators. A doctor by profession, he now carried two guns and was popularly known as Two

Gun Haq. This small town significantly contributed to the fight against the Pakistan army and for the liberation of Bangladesh.

When we arrived in Chuadanga, we found it perfectly at peace—shops were open, and people were in their homes. Dr Haq was going around the town and had his men of Mukti Bahini fighters ready to fight the Pakistan army or the *Razakars*, the paramilitary force Pakistan had raised to create the reign of terror and fear. Dr Haq had confidently declared to me that it would not be easy for Pakistan army to enter Chuadanga.

The fight Dr Haq put up from Chuadanga and the defence of Mukti Bahini posed a challenge to the powerful and heavily armed Pakistan army. East Pakistan was not a small place to be easily captured and controlled. By then, the number of Pakistani soldiers in East Pakistan had risen, crossing over 90,000.

Dr Haq renamed Chuadanga as Joy Bangla, and set up a radio station, and reworked phone lines to India. His contribution to the fight for the liberation of Bangladesh is part of Bangladesh's history. Our coverage showed the world how the people of East Pakistan fought back to create Bangladesh, a country belonging to Bengali-speaking people.

The crackdown by Tikka Khan was not limited just to towns and cities of East Pakistan. The Pakistan army—the paramilitary Razakars—were going into the villages and looting them, irrespective of whether the victims were Hindus or Muslims. There were now more than seven million refugees who had fled to India by July.

Appealing to the Pakistan government had proved to be a waste of time. The world media was now aware of the magnitude of the human problem that India was facing. India realised that the ultimate solution to their problem lay in army action.

India's Prime Minister Mrs Gandhi toured European countries to apprise leaders of Pakistan's actions in East Pakistan, but nothing emerged from this visit. Nevertheless, she did let the US know what its ally Pakistan was doing. It was there for the whole world to see.

As the number of refugees in India reached ten million, the Chief of the Indian Army, Gen Sam Manekshaw, had already been informed of the action required. Pakistan was also aware that India's only option would be to attack East Pakistan and send the refugees back. Pakistan was confident of support from the US in such a scenario. Gen Yahya Khan was confident that his army in East Pakistan could blunt an Indian attack or force a stalemate. He appeared to disregard Tikka Khan's failure in East Pakistan. In Bangladesh, Tikka Khan's crackdown had strengthened the local people's determination to have their own country, Bangladesh. Mukti Bahini's guerilla attacks kept the hope alive.

To keep the US informed of his counterplan, Gen

Yahya Khan kept the local US Chargé d'Affaires in Islamabad, Sydney Sobers, updated. I met Sydney Sobers years later in Washington DC and he told me about Gen Yahya Khan's plans.

Sydney sent his officers to meet Pakistan army officers in Lahore and check the feasibility of Gen Yahya's plans. Sydney recounted that his officers were taken to the border areas, and were entertained, wined and dined in Lahore. These US officers later briefed Sydney that Pakistan's plan was well-prepared and backed with forces. Yahya Khan's plan was to capture Amritsar and move further into India, before stopping at River Beas.

Meanwhile, the world was aware of the miserable state of the refugees from East Pakistan. Several leaders from different countries, including Edward Kennedy, had visited the refugee camps in early August. When Kennedy visited the camps, he experienced firsthand the plight of the refugees during the heavy monsoon rains. He assured the press that he would inform America of the dismal conditions in the refugee camps, and the financial load on India for taking care of nearly ten million men, women and children.

By October, the rains had eased, but the flooded areas and rivers took longer to return to normal condition. India began amassing troops along the frontier with East Pakistan to help the BSF stop any further influx of refugees. Unrest in East Pakistan continued despite the Pakistan army's crackdown and extreme torture of Bengalis by the army, police and the *Razakars*. The local Bengali police had rebelled at many police stations.

Gen Yahya Khan was now certain that India would attack East Pakistan. On the night of 3 December 1971, Khan ordered his air force to attack Indian airbases in the north at Ambala and other places, signifying the launch of his 'Operation Chengiz Khan' meant to preempt any Indian attack in East Pakistan. The name itself suggests a reign of terror and torture which Yahya Khan had created in East Pakistan. Ironically, Chengiz Khan, the ruler of the Mongol Empire, would massacre and torture the people in the areas he captured. Yahya Khan had done exactly that in East Pakistan.

Yahya Khan was surprised to learn that his air force could not do much damage as India was already an attack from West Pakistan. When he launched ground operations, his forces suffered heavy casualties without making any inroads into India. His dream of capturing Amritsar remained a wish that was never fulfilled.

India declared war on 4 December 1971. Indian army outflanked the Pakistan army and moved fast into East Pakistan as well giving them a tough fight with the support of the well-trained Mukti Bahini or Liberation Force of Bangladesh. India announced its formal recognition of the government of Bangladesh and the country. For India, East Pakistan ceased to exist.

The Indian Army had moved fast, knowing that the US could step in to support Pakistan. Nixon had ordered the Nuclear-powered Seventh fleet of the US navy to move to the Bay of Bengal to help Pakistan. India's Navy, with INS Vikrant, carried out air raids on Chittagong and surrounding areas. The Soviet Union, with whom India had signed a Treaty of Friendship, also moved its fleet into the area.

On 14 December, Gen Sam Manekshaw issued an ultimatum to the Pakistan army and its commanders in East Pakistan to either surrender or be ready for annihilation. Pakistan commander Gen Niazi agreed to surrender, following which Maj Gen J F R Jacob flew to Dhaka to finalise the terms of the surrender that Lt Gen J S Arora had organised.

When the war ended, Pakistan had lost over 15,000 km of territory on the Western front, where it was hoping to capture Indian territory. India also liberated over 800 km in Kashmir, including some strategic heights.

On 16 December 1971, I flew to Dhaka when Lt Gen Jagjit Singh Arora and his wife, together with other army officers, flew into Dhaka to sign the surrender document and accept the Pakistan army's surrender. The surrender ceremony took place in public in the Race Course ground, watched by thousands of Bengalis. The Indian Army had ensured the security of Pakistan's officers.

Lt Gen Niazi, commander of Pakistan's 93,000-strong

army, signed the document and formally surrendered to Lt Gen Jagjit Singh Arora. A K Khandkar was present, representing the Bangladesh forces and their provisional government. As Lt Gen Niazi formally took out his revolver and placed it on the table before Gen Aurora, a wild cheer from the assembled crowd rent the air. This was the biggest surrender of any army since the Second World War.

The Pakistan army was allowed to carry its weapons to protect itself from being attacked by the angry people of Bangladesh. They entered military cantonments where the weapons were surrendered to the Indian Army. Pakistan's forces were then moved into POW camps, while Lt Gen Niazi and other senior officers of the Pakistan army were flown to Calcutta.

The provisional government and its leaders flew into Dhaka to take charge of the country. Sheikh Mujibur Rahman returned to Dhaka on 10 January 1972 to a huge welcome. The Awami League had achieved what it set out to do in 1971—to have a Bengali-speaking country, Bangladesh. This was yet another event that changed South Asia by adding another country and splitting Pakistan into two.

Chapter 8

Sri Lanka, a 'Gem in the Indian Ocean', is a country with a long history. It has had various names since its ancient past. The great Indian epic Ramayana, which is played all over South East Asia, has its story set in Lanka. Today, the beautiful country is a huge tourist destination besides being a strategic naval centre in South Asia. Tourists from all over the world visit Sri Lanka for its historic riches and for its pristine beaches.

It can be hot and humid in the plains, but as you move to Sri Lanka's own highlands, you won't find mountains as high as the Himalayas or Alps here. What you do find are lush green plantations of the world-famous Ceylon Tea. The waterfalls here are beautiful and charming in their own right and the weather, pleasant and cool.

When travelling around Sri Lanka, you need not stay in one of the several great hotels. Smaller places are well-developed and may surprise you. The island nation has its own reserve forests. The Sinharaja forest was declared a World Heritage Site by UNESCO. Unlike the forests in India, the Sinharaja forest is well protected. It is a rainforest with a rich biodiversity.

Sri Lanka has a long history. There is controversy among historians about the early immigrants to the country and these are believed to have included Sinhalese-speaking people. Also among early migrants were the Tamils, who set up a Tamil kingdom in Jaffna. The powerful Sinhalese kingdom was based in Anuradhapura. Even today, it is a great place to visit.

Buddhism came to Sri Lanka when the Indian Emperor Ashoka sent his son Mahindra to the island country. Knowing the importance of the island country, Ashoka decided that his son should lead the delegation of the monks. After the huge battle of Kalinga, Emperor Ashoka, who was expanding his empire, returned to the battlefield and was horrified by the killings, injuries and sufferings that he saw. He then decided to adopt Buddha's teachings and give up violence. Buddhism took firm roots in Sri Lanka and continues to be the majority religion there. Ironically, it is hardly practised in India.

Emperor Ashoka also sent monks all over Southeast Asia to spread the message of the Buddha. Thus, we see Buddhism in almost all the countries, barring some where Islam took root, later. The only Hindu island in the Far East is Bali, which is about 95 per cent Hindu. The people there still observe customs that Hindus followed centuries ago.

In the middle centuries, Europeans started moving to new places in the world, looking for opportunities. As in India, the Portuguese were the first to land in Sri Lanka, led by Lourenço de Almeida in 1505. The country was known as Ceylon then. The Portuguese found the country to be important for their expansion into Asia. As they settled, they first built a port, and then a fort, steadily expanding along the coast. The interior was inhabited with several small kingdoms.

The Portuguese settled along the coast of Sri Lanka. Then came the Dutch at the beginning of the seventeenth century, around 1602, led by Joris van Spilbergen.

The Dutch had also landed on the Malabar Coast of India, and were moving towards Africa. Skirmishes and fighting followed as the Dutch tried to expel the Portuguese from Sri Lanka. Nobody wanted any competition.

The Dutch sought an agreement with the Kingdom of Kandy to help expel the Portuguese. It was a smart move to get local support. A series of conflicts followed, and in 1656, the Dutch managed to capture Colombo.

They moved further and finally succeeded in throwing the Portuguese out of Sri Lanka.

Meanwhile, the British were comfortably ensconced across the sea in Madras, a city they had developed along the Southern coast of India. The Dutch presence in Ceylon was managed through the Dutch East India

Company, known as the Vereenigde Oost-Indische Compagnie or VOC.

It must be noted that these European powers were poorer compared to the people of South Asia. During a war with Spain in 1592, the British had captured a Portuguese ship loaded with goods from China and India that were meant to be sold in Europe to rich and royal families. The value of the items, including the spices and fine cotton, were estimated to be almost as good as the treasury of England in those days.

The huge profit made from the spices and fine textiles made many European countries earn riches for its trading families. For the Dutch East India Company, Ceylon's spice wealth was as valuable as India was for the British East India Company. The royal European families desired not just the land's spices, but its fine textiles as well.

The East India Company found the Dutch in Sri Lanka eating into their profits. The Company, had ignored Ceylon so far, but it now decided to use its power to expel the Dutch out of Ceylon. With a strong army of British troops and Indian sepoys, the Company decided to attack the Dutch.

The British began their action in 1796, prompted by Napoleon's capture of the Netherlands in Europe. This had compromised and weakened the position of the Dutch overseas, including in Ceylon.

The Dutch, who were, by then, in full control of

Ceylon, were determined to stay put.

The British naval ships attacked from their base in Madras and, after brief battles at Colombo and Trincomalee, secured the surrender of the Dutch forces. They now wielded power in Ceylon.

The British knew that France too wanted to capture Ceylon because of its strategic location in the Indian Ocean. However, to make Ceylon a part of the British Empire, the British signed the Treaty of Amiens in 1802, by which France recognised Ceylon as a part of the British Empire. Ceylon was declared a Crown Colony.

This event opened the door for a major change in the country, which was soon to be unified and eliminate remaining kingdoms. Kandy was a major hurdle that had to be removed to make movement from East to West within the island nation easy, lay roads and get on with the development of the highlands. Unlike the Ceylonese, the Kandyans did not trust the British. They knew how the British had taken control of South India.

The British started to work on the Kandyan nobles and chiefs who were the main support base of the ruler. It did not take the British long to buy them or win them over. With their help, the British soon had Kandy under their control. However, they had assured the nobles that they would retain their special status and receive financial support from the British. In their fight to gain control over Ceylon, the British had interfered with Buddhist customs.

This led to a popular rebellion in 1818 which the British managed to suppress. With this rebellion foiled, the British firmly settled in Ceylon with Colombo as the capital.

A unified country with strategic value in the Indian Ocean now began to be developed as a single entity. The Tamil-speaking Jaffna region was also brought together with the majority Sinhalese. The two communities lived peacefully in their respective areas. The British followed a divide-and-rule policy between the Sinhalese and Tamils even though both were original inhabitants of Ceylon.

The British worked towards developing the highlands to make them productive and successfully grew coffee pods. A shortage of labour resulted in immigration of Tamils from South India, who came over as indentured labour. Their hard work soon changed the very look of the highlands. The British then started growing tea and soon after, Ceylon tea became world famous. It was a backbreaking task, mostly done by the Tamil men and women. The Sinhalese were not available to work on the plantations.

The British established their infrastructure and government and introduced many social reforms in Ceylon. They did away with bonded labour where one had to work for the money lender without a salary on failing to pay off their debts. Besides developing the highlands, the British helped grow spices and improved agricultural practices.

Political institutions, like legislative and executive

councils, were set up. The British were almost creating a new country out of an island that had tens of small kingdoms.

After creating the right infrastructure for the country's management, judiciary, and economic policy, the British ended monopolies and introduced a capitalist economy of competition. They even set up a small Ceylon Defence Force (CDF).

With education and English governance, there was a rise in the number of well-educated Sinhalese and Tamils who could take up employment. Many of them were now inducted into the government by the British. Nationalist demands also began to rise.

During the First World War, the CDF made its own limited contribution to the war effort. One of the officers of the Ceylon Force, Second Lieutenant Basil Arthur Horsfall was posthumously awarded the Victoria Cross, the highest honour. Ceylon was proud of its people, be it Sinhalese or Tamil.

During the Second World War, after the fall of Singapore, Ceylon gained importance because it ensured that the sea lanes were protected. Lord Mountbatten headed the Southeast Asia Command from Kandy. The Royal Navy and Royal Air Force were also based in Colombo to ensure that the sea lanes were secured for the Allied Forces in their fight against the Japanese.

The Japanese had used British and Indian POWs and officers to build a railway bridge over the Kwai in Thailand.

Again, it was from here that a strategy was developed to blow up the bridge before the Japanese could advance further. The bridge still exists in Thailand and can be seen by tourists visiting the country.

By the Second World War, Ceylon had made huge progress. However, ethnic differences between Sinhalese and Tamils were growing as the British pursued their divide-and-rule policy. Sinhalese were in the majority and used it against the Tamils in the Council.

Following India's independence in 1947, Ceylon gained independence on 4 February 1948, and was now the Dominion of Ceylon. Its first Prime Minster was D S Senanayake while Sir Henry Monck-Mason Moore became the Governor General.

As time progressed, a deep national fervour gripped the Sinhalese.

Senanayake's United National Party (UNP) was dominated by British-educated leaders who wanted to develop Ceylon as the Great Britain of the East. In 1955, UNP was defeated by the Sri Lanka Freedom Party (SLFP) and SWRD Bandaranaike was elected the Prime Minister of Ceylon.

Prime Minister Bandaranaike declared Sinhalese as the sole official language of Ceylon. This had been among his populist slogans to win Sinhalese support. The relations between the Sinhalese majority and Tamil-speaking minority immediately began to sour because of this policy. This meant that Tamils would not be able to join government services and have problems in education as Sinhalese was the language of governance. The policy also estranged the small Christian population.

SLFP also changed the country's economic policy from capitalist to socialist, which resulted in rising prices and a fall in the value of Ceylon's currency as imports of consumer goods surpassed exports. On 25 September 1959, Bandaranaike was assassinated by a Buddhist monk Talduwe Somarama Thero who fired at him. Bandaranaike died the next day.

SWRD Bandaranaike was succeeded by his widow Sirimavo Bandaranaike, who thus became the world's first woman Prime Minister. She introduced policies to placate the Buddhist community, and took steps to minimise the role of Christian Missionaries in education.

The Dominion status of Ceylon was changed in 1972 when the country decided to become a republic, and was renamed as Sri Lanka. The first President of the country was William Gopallawa.

With the relations between the Sinhala majority and Tamils worsening, Tamils decided to stake a demand for the separate country of Jaffna. Hundreds of Tamils, particularly from the tea plantations, began to leave the country and go as refugees to India's Tamil Nadu. Failing to crush Tamil militants in Jaffna, the Sri Lankan government decided to stop movement of goods to Jaffna to starve the population and force the militants to surrender.

Tamil Nadu in South India raged over the ill-treatment meted out to the Tamil-speaking minority in Sri Lanka. The government, headed by President Junius Richard Jayewardene, failed to accept India's requests to lift the blockade of Jaffna.

India was left with no option but to airdrop food in Jaffna, which enraged Sri Lanka and the Sinhalese-speaking people. After discussions between the two governments, India's Prime Minister Rajiv Gandhi flew to Colombo. I was part of his press party.

After discussions, an accord was signed between Sri Lanka's President Jayawardene and Indian Prime Minister Rajiv Gandhi.

Prime Minister Gandhi now came out to inspect a Guard of Honour by the Sri Lankan naval force. A Naval guard, Vijitha Rohana de Silva made an assassination attempt on the Indian Prime Minister. I was walking beside him covering the inspection when this happened. Rajiv Gandhi, was able to dodge the attempt, as described earlier in the book.

This visit by one of India's finest Prime Ministers led to several repercussions such as the Indian Peace Keeping Force being unable to disarm or win over the Tamil militant group LTTE, which had huge support from Sri Lankan Tamils all over the world. The continuous financial support to LTTE by thousands of rich Sri Lankan Tamils settled abroad helped the LTTE carry on the fight for separation in Sri Lanka.

LTTE leader V Prabhakaran and his colleagues resented Rajiv Gandhi. While campaigning for India's 1991 elections, Rajiv Gandhi arrived at Sriperumbudur in Tamil Nadu. As he walked towards the dais acknowledging his supporters, an LTTE woman suicide bomber standing among them triggered off a bomb as he approached her, killing him on the spot. India lost a great man that day. This tragic event had far-reaching impact on Indian politics.

It took a long time for Sri Lanka's forces to defeat the LTTE. It was only in May 2009 that the LTTE was finally defeated and their leader V Prabhakaran killed. The forces that sought a separate country for Tamil-speaking people are all gone now. Sri Lanka now has to limp back to peace.

The government of Sri Lanka amended its language policy in 1987 recognising Tamil also as an official language and English as a link language. This long-delayed action brought Sri Lankan Tamils back into the mainstream as equals. Decades of violence and the virtual civil war unleashed by Bandaranaike's Sinhalese-only language policy finally came to an end and peace returned to Sri Lanka.

Sri Lanka's economy has been precarious from its very birth as an independent country. Though the British left comfortable reserves, imports of essentials and consumer goods soon began to strain the country. Earnings from exports were limited to spices, tea, tourism and remittances from Sri Lankans working abroad. The imports and development work became dependent on foreign loans, including those from the IMF.

Then came the proverbial last straw on the camel's back. The world was hit by the Covid epidemic in 2019. Tourism came to a halt, as the world locked down. Sri Lanka was already suffering from a shortage of petroleum goods. As the economy began to collapse, mass demonstrations erupted against the government. Amid the economic crisis and demonstrations, the Rajapaksa government fell in July 2022.

Loans by some countries given to Sri Lanka, notably by China, are now an integral part of their foreign policy and can be described as a form of diplomacy of bringing nations under a debt-trap. In this case, China secured a 99-years lease of Sri Lanka's Hambantota International Port. The loss of this port meant a loss of revenue. Sri Lanka has a busy sea route, used by most freight ships going towards the Suez Canal and further into Europe.

Finally, Sri Lanka managed to get a bailout loan from the IMF. India too pitched in with support to Sri Lanka. The country is now once again on the road to development.

Chapter 9

Maldives is located in the Indian ocean, a country of about 1,200 islands, of which only around 200 are inhabited. These islands are as beautiful as the coral reefs themselves. The water in the sea around here looks blue due to the bright sunlight and the coral reefs in the area. The island country is spread over about 800 kilometres from North to South, while the distance from East to West is around 130 kilometres. The closest cluster of islands lies about 600 km southwest of India's mainland. The capital of the country is Malé. From India's Southern mainland coast, Cochin, in Kerala is more than 700 km away. The closest Indian territory is Lakshadweep Islands.

The earliest settlers here came from South India and Sri Lanka. Over time, a mixed population of Maldivians has evolved who speak the Dhivehi language. English is also widely spoken and is used in business and government, in addition to Dhivehi.

The economy of Maldives is dependent upon tourism. Fishing and boat-building have been traditional businesses. In recent years, efforts have been made to attract foreign investment and industries.

The strategic location of these islands attracted Europeans as they looked for trading partners. With its booming economy based on spices and fine textiles, India was a major attraction. The Portuguese were the first Europeans to land in India, and soon, they began looking for other areas to explore and found Sri Lanka and the Maldivian Islands. The Portuguese captured some of the islands along the coast of Ceylon.

As time passed, Maldives also became part of the British Empire, as did India and Ceylon. India gained independence on 15 August 1947. Ceylon became free on 4 February 1948. The British stayed in Maldives longer because of its strategic importance in a world hit by the Cold War. Maldives gained independence only on 26 July 1965. Prior to this, Maldives was a British protectorate.

From 1796, when the East India Company operated from Bombay, the Company ensured the protection of its sea routes by bringing Maldives under UK's protection. But it was only in 1885, under the rule of Queen Victoria, that Maldives' monarch Muhammed Mueenuddeen II officially accepted British protection. This led to many of the Maldivian King's powers being transferred to the Prime Minister in running the country's government.

During the Second World War, Britain's Royal Air Force had a base on Gan Island, which later became the country's international airport. The Gan base rendered significant service during the war. Supply routes were kept open, and fighter aircraft and other long-distance planes could refuel at Gan. Now it is a busy international airport bringing in tourists from all over the world to see the country's famed beaches.

A major change came to the Maldives in March 1968 when it held a referendum that resulted in the abolition of the monarchy. Ibrahim Nasir became the first President of the Republic.

India's relations with Maldives have been very friendly. There was once a contentious issue regarding Minicoy Island, with Maldives laying claim to it. However, it was resolved after mutual discussions, and the two countries signed a Maritime Boundary Treaty in 1976 with Maldives recognising Minicoy as an integral part of India.

In 1988, Maldivian dissidents opposed to President Maumoon Gayoom staged a rebellion led by Abdullah Luthufi who had hired mercenaries from the People's Liberation Organisation of Tamil Eelam (PLOTE), a Sri Lankan militant group. India gave prompt military assistance to President Gayoom under Operation Cactus. The country first sent paratroopers to take control of the airport to help airborne troops to land. The operation was executed with great speed, and the capital city, Malé, was quickly secured by troops.

Once Malé had been secured and President Gayoom rescued, Indian troops went in to capture the coup plotters. The mercenaries tried to flee to Sri Lanka on a captured ship, but the Indian Navy blocked the attempt and captured the mercenaries and their leaders.

The prompt assistance that India provided to Maldives President Gayoom led to the development of trust and friendly relations between the two countries. India withdrew its troops immediately after Operation Cactus concluded, ensuring there was no fear within the Maldives government regarding Indian dominance.

India again came to the rescue of Maldives in 2004 when it suffered severe damage from the tsunami that also hit South India. President Gayoom sought global help, and India responded immediately with help arriving in naval ships, aircraft and helicopters which also conducted search and rescue operations across the scattered islands. Some islands had to be completely given up for habitation as these had been submerged by the tsunami waves. The entire population was thereby moved to another island. India provided medical relief, food supplies and drinking water along with the Red Cross that also arrived with a large team to facilitate assistance and rebuilding.

President Gayoom ruled over the Maldives for almost thirty years. He eventually lost the 2008 elections to Mohamed Nasheed. India's relations with Maldives continued to be close and friendly, as they had been earlier.

Meanwhile, the balance of power was changing in the world. China was emerging as an ambitious country, seeing itself replacing the global position held by the USA as the world's most powerful nation. India, though slow, had a growing economy and a powerful defence force well-armed with long-range missiles and modern weaponry. Its navy had expanded to secure the Indian Ocean region for the country. China meanwhile was making its own moves to dominate the sea lanes of the Indian Ocean.

Realising the challenge of a changing world scene, the Indian government devoted its time and resources to strengthening India's defence forces. It emphasised on indigenous weapons production. The Defence Research and Development Organisation (DRDO) was given a free hand not just to match global developments but to go a step further and innovate its own weapons.

Maldives' economy had seen a downturn following the Covid pandemic. Tourism came to a standstill. India sent help to Maldives with a medical team and medicines. It provided over 6 tonnes of hospital supplies and essential medicines, along with food grains, under Operation Sanjeevani. It must be remembered that India, itself, was hit by Covid and was looking after its huge population.

China opened its Embassy in Maldives in 2011, while Maldives had opened its embassy in Beijing in 2009. Every time Maldives faced a problem, such as the drinking water crisis of 2004 in Malé when the island's water treatment plant broke down, it was India that had come to its rescue. The two nations share historical ties, but silently and steadily, China was working on a section of Maldivian society to cultivate support. Eventually, this led to the emergence of a small pro-China lobby working against India. Maldives is one of those few countries in the world that allow visa-free entry to the holders of a Chinese passport.

When Maldives was in urgent need of rebuilding its infrastructure, it started borrowing funds from abroad much like Sri Lanka. China became the largest lender to Maldives. China, as is well-known, uses loans as a means of putting economic pressure on the nations that borrow from them. The example of Sri Lanka leasing the Hambantota port for 99 years to China is a prime example of this practice. Several African nations have suffered the same fate.

This Chinese 'aid-by-loans' policy is now known as China's 'loan diplomacy'. Maldives owes China over US $ 1.3 billion, a huge amount for the Maldivian economy that had suffered a serious setback during the Covid epidemic. This amount of debt can affect the economic sovereignty of Maldives.

In his populist campaign during the 2023 Presidential elections in Maldives, its current President, Mohamed Muizzu, had emphasised economic reforms, anti-corruption measures and national sovereignty. He also wanted foreign military presence to end in his country. This was specifically aimed at India which had about fifty military technicians stationed there to look after helicopters and other assets used by the Maldivian government. Muizzu's campaign reflected his views on India and these were not friendly.

On his swearing-in ceremony as President of Maldives, India had sent its senior cabinet minister Kiren Rijiju, but soon after taking charge as President, the first country that Muizzu chose to visit was China on 7 January 2014. On his return, he reportedly stated that though Maldives was a small nation, it should not be subjected to bullying. It is unclear to which country he was referring to.

During his populist election campaign, Muizzu had assured the people of removing foreign military presence in Maldives. This was an obvious reference to India. India had given some helicopters and planes to Maldives, and a small group from India maintained these helicopters and planes. India recalled these men after Muizzu was elected.

The relations of Maldives with the USA also suffered a setback following Muizzu's election. The USA has been on friendly terms with Maldives since its independence and have several agreements, including one on defence cooperation. Ever since Muizzu's election, the United States has been wary of Maldives' relations with China.

In recent times, President Muizzu has sought to

revive friendly relations with India and visited India in October 2024. India agreed to assist Maldives with US $ 750 million in a currency swap agreement. Several other agreements were also signed.

During his stay in Delhi, President Muizzu also sought revival of Indian tourists visiting Maldives, which had suffered a setback during a social media campaign calling for a boycott of Maldives following the pro-China and anti-India rhetoric during his election campaign. The two countries also issued a vision statement for comprehensive economic and maritime security. It was clear that President Muizzu was keen on reviving friendly relations with India.

However, China's presence in South Asia, cannot be ignored.

Chapter 10

Like other South Asian countries, Burma is an ancient land and has and is believed to have a prehistoric history. The earliest recorded development known to historians in the region is the emergence of the Kingdom of Pagan in 849 AD. There is a Pagan-era pagoda, or its prototype, at Sri Ksetra. Burma was a transit country in China and India trade. This connection with India, brought Buddhism to Burma.

The Shan people of Burma entered the region during the early Mongol attacks on Burmese kingdoms. Many stayed on and flourished. One of the later kingdoms, Mrauk-U, became powerful and included parts of Bangladesh in the fifteenth and seventeenth centuries.

India's relationship with Burma goes into the historic past when Orissa was known as Kalinga, the kingdom that Asoka attacked. Historian and author Dr Benudhar Patra has made an excellent study of Kalinga's prosperity and the country's relations with Burma. Kalinga was a prosperous country because of its maritime trade. It had a number of medieval ports, the famous ones being at Khalkattapatna, Kalingapatnam, Pitunda and Palur.

Dr Patra writes that Kalinga had maintained close trade contact with Burma (Myanmar) in ancient times. Kautilya's *Arthashastra* of the early Mauryan period refers to Burma as *Suvarnabhumi* or the golden land. When I visited Burma, I prayed at the Shwedagon Pagoda, which is said to have relics, in the form of eight hairs, of Lord Budha.

The British fought three wars to take control of Burma. In the first war, in 1824, the East India Company took control of North-East India. The Burmese rulers too were keen on expanding their territory into North-East India, but the war ended with Britain gaining control of Assam, Manipur and other areas. They also captured the Arakan province and adjoining territories. A naval attack was launched on Rangoon (now Yangon) in May 1824 resulting in the British victory. It was a very rich city, and the East India Company soldiers and officers looted the city. However, the war cost the Company heavily both in terms of manpower and the amount spent in this aggressive war. However, they had achieved their objective—of capturing Burma.

The Konbaung Dynasty of Burma was strong and had become the dominant power in South-East Asia and accordingly, they wanted Arakan, Assam and other areas which the British ruled. Lord Dalhousie, Governor General of British India was equally ambitious and wanted to extend British control into Burma. By the end of the war in 1885, Dalhousie had captured the Burmese province of Pegu and other timber-rich areas, including lower Burma.

The third war started when the British heard of King Thibaw seeking an alliance with the French just as Tipu Sultan had done in South India. The British attacked with full force, capturing Mandalay, the capital of Burma and annexed Burma into the Indian Empire. The Burmese people were dissatisfied with Burma being a province of India. This led to a national movement against the British. Burma was another British Colony that was robbed of its riches.

The first War in Burma by the East India Company saw a mutiny by its 47th Regiment of Bengal Infantry in India. The sepoys refused to board the ships and travel to Burma. First, it was against a Hindu edict to cross the ocean. Second, the sepoys had heard stories of the strong Burmese Empire and its fighting capabilities that had caused heavy casualties to the British.

The mutiny of 1857, also known as India's first war of independence, saw the end of the Mughal Dynasty in India. The last Mughal Poet-emperor Bahadur Shah Zafar, was put on trial at Red Fort, divested of his rule, and sent off with his wives and staff to Rangoon, a far-off corner of the British Indian Empire.

In Punjab, the British had built canals through the barren lands of Punjab for the farmers around Jalandhar. The British used to recruit Sikh soldiers and other Punjabis from this region. The farmers worked hard on the barren land and turned it into a fertile agricultural land. Years later, when the British wanted to take away the fertile lands, a major agitation by the farmers, led by Ajit Singh, uncle of the revolutionary Bhagat Singh, took place. The agitation was known as *Pagdi sambhal Jatta* or Save your honour, Jatt. Ajit Singh was arrested and externed to the farthest corner of India—to Mandalay prison in Burma. Lala Lajpat Rai, another Punjabi leader, was also sent there. The British were using Burma to imprison Indian revolutionaries.

With the dawn of the twentieth century, the simmering anger against British rule became a call for independence. Open protests against British rule were led by students in Burma. Suppression by the British resulted in more protests, with some of them turning violent. As in India, the education system in Burma had created British-produced clerks for government service, with some reaching slightly higher positions. To the credit of these new Burmese leaders, they first devoted their attention to protecting their culture and religion. The Young Men's Buddhist Association (YMBA) was formed as a result.

The Second World War saw the Japanese defeat and

push the British out of Burma, which was then declared an independent country. A Burmese government was installed under Dr Ba Maw as Prime Minister and head. Thakin Nu, or U Nu as he was popularly known, was the minister for foreign affairs. Another tall Burmese leader, General Aung San, was the minister for defence and also the Deputy Prime Minister.

The Burmese leaders soon realised that the independence announced by the Japanese was a smokescreen, as the Japanese army continued to interfere and exploit Burma's resources, including agricultural products. This resulted in Aung San, who had first supported the Japanese, allying with the British once again. U Nu also resigned.

The defeat of the Indian National Army and the Japanese in the fiercely fought battle of Imphal soon turned the tables. The INA and the Japanese had to retreat under the very difficult conditions of monsoon and disease. Subhas Chandra Bose though ensured that women soldiers of the INA were safely sent back home.

The Japanese finally surrendered to the Allied Forces on 2 September 1945 after Japanese areas of Hiroshima and Nagasaki were bombed by the Americans. The bombs made the Japanese feel as if the US had issued a warning—if they did not surrender, they would disappear like Hiroshima and Nagasaki had.

Meanwhile, in Burma, as the colonial power

regained control, the military administration and the pre-war government insisted that Aung San be put on trial for collaborating with the Japanese. However, Lord Mountbatten, realising Aung San's hold on the Burmese people, did not allow it and Aung San took charge as Prime Minister of Burma on 27 March 1945.

By now, Britain was not just a tired nation but also nearly bankrupt. It needed a huge amount of money to rebuild the damage suffered during the Second World War. The British had repeatedly told Indian leaders that independence would come to India after the war. With Churchill gone, his successor Clement Attlee began negotiations to transfer power. Finally, India became free on 15 August 1947, albeit with a partition.

Negotiations then began for Burma's independence. Aung San led the negotiations as leader of the Anti-Fascist People's Freedom League. Aung San and his colleagues travelled to London to finalise the negotiations with Prime Minister Clement Attlee. The British agreed to leave Burma, and the country was to be independent. On his return, Aung San convened a meeting of the Constituent Assembly and Burma decided to leave the British Commonwealth of Nations.

A huge tragedy, however, hit Burma when Aung San and some of his cabinet colleagues were assassinated on 19 July 1947. Burma continues to suffer in the aftermath of this assassination, which was carried out by gunmen sent by a former Prime Minister U Saw.

The Constituent Assembly elected Shwe Thaik as the provisional President of Burma. Meanwhile, the British Parliament concluded its discussions and passed the Independence Act of Burma on 10 December 1947. Burma achieved independence on 4 January 1948. U Nu became the first Prime Minister of independent Burma.

It was not easy to rule Burma, as the country had suffered terrible destruction during the Second World War when the Japanese moved in after defeating the British and later, when the Allies pushed the Japanese out of Burma. The country was in urgent need of internal peace. U Nu adopted a policy of non-alignment for his government that amounted to neutrality.

Meanwhile, U Nu was facing serious internal problems. The communists were the first insurgents who did not accept the U Nu government. Then came disgruntled leaders who were colleagues of Aung San. The Karens, an ethnic minority in the plains, wanted to be free and independent of Burma.

Neighbouring China had its own set of troubles. Chiang Kai-shek's government had been pushed out by Mao Tse Tung (also spelled as Zedong). While retreating, several of the army contingents of Chiang Kai-shek entered Burma and occupied areas of the Shan Plateau. Burma, having already recognised Mao's China, refused to accept any aid from the USA until these forces surrendered to the Burmese army.

With concerted efforts, the U Nu government established some internal peace and the work of rebuilding the Burmese economy started. Expecting a possible threat to his government, U Nu requested Gen Ne Win, who was second in command to Aung San, to take charge as the Prime Minister and restore order and peace in the country. In the 1962 General Elections, in a peaceful Burma, U Nu was returned to office with an absolute majority.

However, in March 1962, Ne Win led a military coup, and arrested U Nu and several of his cabinet colleagues. He also arrested the Chief Justice of Burma. Suspending the Constitution, he established a single-party, military-controlled Socialist Burma. Ne Win tried to run a Communist style economy whereby he nationalised all private businesses. All this did not improve the economy, but there was no way that the public could seek redressal.

Upon release, U Nu, a devout Buddhist, spent most of his time preaching Buddhism. He tried politically to regain power, but the military was firmly in the saddle. He kept himself occupied with his literary work and passed away at the age of eighty-seven on 14 February 1995.

The only challenge to the military rulers of Burma came from Aung San's daughter, Aung San Suu Kyi. She was living in England with her British husband, Michael Aris and her two children. In 1988, she decided to visit Burma, primarily to look after her ailing mother. Once there, she met several associates of her late father and formed the National League for Democracy (NLD) with their support. In the 1990 General Elections, NLD had a landslide victory, winning 80 per cent of the Parliament.

The military refused to hand over power. Suu Kyi was detained. She tried nonviolent methods to try and convince that Burma belonged to its people. She even held various offices as a member of another party, the Pyithu Hluttaw.

In April 2016, Aung San Suu Kyi became a State Counsellor, an office equal to that of the Prime Minster. It was during her tenure that the military carried out a genocide against the Rohingya Muslims. Survivors fled to Bangladesh. Some made their way to India through either Bangladesh or Pakistan. India has been trying to expel these illegal immigrants ever since. Suu Kyi was criticised all over the world for not taking any action to protect the Rohingyas. However, she defended the military action at the International Court of Justice.

Suu Kyi had received the Nobel Prize in 1991 for her non-violent, peaceful struggle against the army rule. Ironically, after becoming a State Counsellor in 2016, she was now defending the same military.

As a popular leader of Burma, Suu Kyi won the 2020 General Elections easily, but was arrested in another coup against her. There were widespread protests across the country and students came out on the streets defying military brutality. Suu Kyi was sent to prison for four years. The military filed all kinds of charges against her, and sentenced her to thirty-three years in prison. The world, including the UN, condemned the military junta. This is the sad story of Burma, where the military and select businessmen flourish while the common man lives in poverty. China has kept a close watch on the country. India has an embassy in Yangon (Rangoon) and a Consulate in Mandalay. The government functions from Naypyidaw, a new city they built from scratch.

The military rulers have never explained what they did to Aung San Suu Kyi. Naypyidaw is more centrally and strategically located for administration than Rangoon. The city is like a military cantonment, where the rulers do not have to face any unruly civilians. What is the future for the beautiful country of Burma? Only time will tell.

Chapter 11

The USA is trying to retrieve its role as the world's most powerful nation, both financially and militarily. 'Make America Great Again' (MAGA) was part of Donald Trump's election campaign. To start with, President Donald Trump did away with a well-established system of global trading under the World Trade Organization (WTO). Trump accused other nations of imposing discriminatory tariffs against the USA. He has also imposed high tariffs on America's close neighbour, Canada.

Many say that Trump's drive to enforce his ideas on world trade could well have a disastrous effect on the American economy by giving US citizens a high rate of inflation. It is too early to say that. However, the pressure Donald Trump has placed on world trade has succeeded in questions being raised on the rule-based trading system. The challenge that the United States faces is that many other countries, specifically China and India, have progressed in manufacturing industries and technology, something in which the US earlier dominated the world.

China's Belt and Road Initiative is a major project launched in 2013 to ensure connectivity and trade for China through a network of enhanced infrastructure such as railways, ports, pipelines and highways. It will connect Asia, Europe and Africa thus expanding China's economic, political and strategic influence in these regions. Global powers have objected to this, even as China scouts around looking for South Asian countries to influence. As part of its Belt and Road project, China needs various infrastructure projects in countries like Sri Lanka, Maldives, Nepal and Bangladesh. Bangladesh has become vulnerable since its textile exports are not faring well. The Belt and Road initiative will ultimately be a debt trap for supporting nations and is destined to fail.

Even though China needs infrastructure in some of the South Asian countries, it does not develop them at its own cost, but instead offers the carrot of employment and economic possibilities that such an infrastructure would create. Once a nation agrees, China usually offers them loans at a relatively high rate of interest, which can then lead to a debt-trap. It is already known in international circles as China's 'debt-trap diplomacy'.

A nation's inability to repay such loans can even affect its sovereignty. Sri Lanka and now Maldives have already fallen victims to this debt-trap diplomacy and it remains to be seen whether such high-interest loans have given any advantage to Sri Lanka's economy especially when it gave up all rights to its historic deep-sea port of Hambantota to China on a 99-year lease.

At the Hambantota port, a Chinese petroleum Company has taken over the business of refuelling ships and handling oil tank projects. In ancient times, Hambantota was part of the sea Silk Route, and today, the port is an important part of China's Belt and Road project.

China is doing this, not just in South Asia, but in many other regions of the world. The People's Republic of China was a sleeping giant during the Mao era in terms of economic development. In that era, the country was opened for tourists for a one-day visit from Hong Kong via Macau, which was still a Portuguese colony. When I visited it back then, I was shocked to see the conditions in the mainland—dirty roads, every one dressed in Mao suits commuting on bicycles. At the Friendship store, I found salesmen dozing behind dusty showcases.

Following Henry Kissinger's visit to China in 1971 and President Nixon's visit in 1972, relations between the two countries stabilised. It is doubtful if Nixon and Kissinger, who considered himself a great diplomat, realised the consequences of what they offered China in terms of huge investments, technology transfer, and goods manufacturing opportunities.

Today, retail stores all over the US are full of 'Made in

China' products—toys, clothing, watches and electronics. Nixon and Kissinger had expected that once China gets into business mode with the West, it would opt for democracy and give up communism. On the contrary, Communist China has successfully adopted a market economy without affecting its ideology in any manner.

China now exports its goods to every country in the world and its economy is now based on exports rather than domestic consumption. In some South-East Asian countries, I have come across full-fledged Chinese markets where almost everything available is made in China. If President Donald Trump wants to see indigenous goods flood US stores, he must realise that it was the USA that gave China the technology transfer to become a factory of the world. It is widely acknowledged that Nixon and Henry Kissinger's main objective in offering huge investments to China was their hope that by doing so, they would be able to wean China away from the Soviet Union.

In that, Nixon and Kissinger succeeded. But, China began to not only attract American companies to invest in China, but also encouraged them to offer technology transfers to China so that they could get cheap Chinese-made products. Soon, American stores were filled with consumer goods, from toys and clothing to household items for daily use. Today, China dominates the American retail market and challenges the USA in the question of its global stature. China's economy is based on exports and in that, it has achieved great success. It considers itself as a major economic and military power, competing against the USA which has dominated the world for long and considers itself to be doing so even today.

China's approach in South Asia is well-planned. A public-relations drive creates an atmosphere in which local friendly voices are influenced to support Chinese proposals. This is followed by Chinese foreign direct investment, something that most South Asian countries welcome. China builds infrastructure for the country, holding the promise of employment opportunity and new industry. Only much later may a country realise the impact of high-interest loans which they may fail to repay on time.

China has made considerable investments even in India, totalling over US $ 3.2 billion. These investments have been in various sectors, notably electronics, mobile phones, and automobiles. India, too, has made investments in China, with leading Indian companies setting up manufacturing operations in pharmaceuticals and information technology. All major Indian companies have their presence in China.

The balance of payments presently is highly favourable to China, but still India can manage.

Nepal had been a closed country through the Rana period. It was only after King Tribhuvan managed his escape from the palace to India in November 1950 that a political change was ushered in. By the time he returned to Nepal, it had been decided that the Rana Dynasty's rule in Nepal would end. This ultimately led to the end of the Rana rule and of the idea of King Tribhuvan taking charge again of his own country.

Nepal's relations with its immediate neighbour, India, have been brotherly. Nepal is a Hindu country. People of Nepal can come and work in India, as they do in large numbers. China came into the picture after it annexed Tibet and the Dalai Lama took refuge in India. Nepal's borders were now with both India and China as Tibet was now part of China.

China built a large embassy in Kathmandu, and within a very short period, the Communist Party of Nepal became a formidable force to reckon with. Then began a steady campaign against India. Ever since the end of the Rana regime, Nepal's growth has been phenomenal with Indian support. Private businesses grew, tourism developed, star-category hotels opened and casinos opened as well. India continues to be a major partner of Nepal, despite its political ups and downs. Citizens of both countries do not need visas, and can work, seek employment or do business without restrictions. Nepal too has been wise in not accepting loans from China, relying instead on other international institutions.

But with Maldives, China has made rapid progress and has made a big entry there in recent years. The Maldives now owes approximately US $ 1.5 billion to China, a huge sum for that tiny country. The Maldives had always had close relations with India, until the election of President Muizzu, who won on an 'India out' campaign. China might have been the first country he chose to visit, but soon, Muizzu saw sense and sought to repair his country's relationship with India.

Prime Minister Modi also visited the Maldives in July 2025 and was warmly welcomed by President Muizzu. The Maldives President reportedly thanked India for helping his country in dealing with economic problems, including liquidity challenges. The Prime Minister's visit helped reset the relationship between India and the Maldives. India agreed to a fresh line of credit amounting to Rs 4,850 crores and to reduce the annual repayment amount of loans taken earlier by Maldives. Whether India has managed to get Maldives out of the shackles of China, only time will tell.

The relationship between China and Bangladesh is also interesting. Bangladesh emerged after the victory of the Indian Army and of the Mukti Bahini over Pakistan in the 1971 war. East Pakistan was gone and Bangladesh was born. China, however, continued to veto Bangladesh's membership of the UN until 1974, primarily because of its relationship with Pakistan. China's close strategic relationship with Pakistan was forged after the 1962 war with India.

Once China recognised Bangladesh, it made every effort to bring it into its diplomacy debt-trap. It allowed duty-free access for almost all Bangladeshi products into China from 2020. China, however, overlooked the fact that Bangladesh was its strong competitor in garment exports. However, imports of Chinese goods into Bangladesh far exceeded Bangladesh's export to China. And Bangladesh had to take loans from China to meet the deficit.

China has now gone into defence cooperation with Bangladesh, as it has with Pakistan. Bangladesh had imported Chinese weapons, only to find these to be sub-standard. With the fall of Sheikh Hasina and emergence of Mohammed Yunus as the de facto ruler of Bangladesh, with the title of Chief Advisor, there has been a shift in the political scenario. Yunus has close links with the US, where he had lived before flying into Dhaka after the fall of Sheikh Hasina.

Ignoring the hitherto close relations Bangladesh has had with India, Yunus decided to make his first visit to Beijing, where he was warmly welcomed. China offered an investment of more than a billion dollars to Bangladesh. Could this well be a part of China's 'debt diplomacy'?

Yunus later met India's Prime Minister Narendra Modi on the sidelines of a regional meeting in Bangkok. The attacks on the Hindu minority population in Bangladesh, which Yunus has failed to control, have strained Indo-Bangladesh relations. At the same time, anti-India elements in Bangladesh have also been encouraged. Yunus has described India's North East as 'landlocked'. Meanwhile, within Bangladesh, its politically conscious people are clamouring for elections. The people want to see him out or win an election to legitimise his position, which would again change the political scenario in the country.

This is the present-day situation of South Asia vis a vis China. The US also wants to enter into the picture. Meanwhile, India is emerging as a strong military power as was proved recently through its Operation Sindoor, a response to the terror attack in Pahalgam in which twenty-six innocent persons were killed. India retaliated by destroying key terror centres spread all over Pakistan, including in Muridke near Lahore. Pakistan's drones and missiles failed, as these were destroyed by India's air defence system. Indian missiles then destroyed Pakistan's airbases spread across the country. Chinese-made air defence systems and other weapons did not help Pakistan in the short four-day war.

India has been importing a lot of defence armaments from Russia, and its own armaments industry is rapidly developing under government policies encouraging self-reliance and an *Atmanirbhar Bharat*.

India is a rising economic power, and at present is the world's fastest growing economy. This places a huge responsibility on India to ensure friendly relations with all its South Asian neighbours.

India continues to meet the Chinese challenge in South Asia with full force. Pakistan continues to be unstable with its economy in shambles. Pakistan's elected Prime Minister, Imran Khan, is in jail and as a country, it is run by the army. Strange as it may sound, Pakistan's army is also the single largest business owner in Pakistan under the aegis of the Fauji Foundation. Balochistan wants separation, and so does the province of Pakhtunkhwa, previously North West Frontier Province.

South Asia is in turmoil in 2026. China has positioned itself strongly at Hambantota port of Sri Lanka, and now controls a strategic deep-sea port. Bangladesh has a pro-US ruler in Mohammed Yunus. The Nepal government that was sympathetic towards China has fallen due to several reasons. Afghanistan is ruled by the Taliban. Pakistan, a close ally of the US, plays a fine balancing game allowing China to use Gwadar port while also keeping the US happy. Burma continues to be ruled by the military, and remains a secluded country. In the midst of all this, India is the only country peacefully progressing.

South Asia could be facing a challenging time ahead. The silver lining is that the India-US trade deal is done. India now enjoys the lowest US tariffs as compared to its competitors like Vietnam and Bangladesh in areas like textiles. It was a difficult period, but India appears to have surmounted the worst.

The challenge before South Asia centre around

weaponisation as nations will try to get the most sophisticated weapons from any source. The manner in which the American Delta Force destroyed the body guards of the Venezuelan Dictator Maduro is a case in point. Will we see weapons of which no one has heard of? If countries get hold of such weapons, it could change the geopolitics of the region. Is South Asia going to see an Arms Race and be a battle ground for high technology weapons supplied by the US and China? Is this the region where the US and China will jostle for the ultimate sphere of influence?